In God's Waiting Room

Barbara Morello O'Donnell

And

Howard Rankin PhD

DEDICATION

This book is dedicated, in loving memory, to my mother Elizabeth Jay. I wish she could have seen that her years of prayer for me were not in vain. Her accomplishments in art as well as her consistent faith in prayer and belief in mission work will continue to be an inspiration to me. She is greatly missed.

I love you mom.

TABLE OF CONTENTS

ACKNOWLEDGEMENTS

I would like to acknowledge my husband Mike, my son Chris, my sister Carla, and her husband Dino for the loving and constant care during my fourteen-day coma and hospital recovery. Their impeccable care and dedication kept me going in spite of my near-death experience and seemingly hopeless prognosis.

Mike, whose background includes the titles of ER nurse, paramedic, and firefighter, joined forces with my sister Carla, who is also a paramedic, to become my advocates and caregivers along with the hospital medical staff. Mike's two daughters, Shannon and Kristen, were also loving and supportive.

Mike's sister Kathleen and brother-in-law Keith, along with their three children Kevin, Kyle, and Kaleigh, were by my side and made my recovery that much easier.

Special friends Donald and Sharon gave me love and support.

Others who were by my side with love and support include very good friends and fellow reiners from the Sheridan Oak Stables: Kim and Dave, Mike and Marylyn, George and Patty, Margie, Linda, Heath, and Helen.

The hospital staff was also wonderful and supportive, especially to my loved ones who suffered pain and sorrow. Several nurses went beyond the call of duty during my recovery. They played an important part in helping me cope with the traumatic events by just being there for me and calming my nerves. I'll forever remember the simple acts; like holding my hand, taking me to the cafeteria or hair salon, or even just outside for some fresh air.

I would also like to acknowledge Gene Cryer, Brittany MacArthur, Joel Ann Shiffer, Grace Perez, and Mike O'Donnell for their contribution as editors in different phases of the book. Kerry Wohlstein deserves many thanks as well for her contribution on researching the do's and don'ts for coma patients.

I am grateful for the hands-on spiritual leadership and teaching from Chaplain Laura Dahne and Tessie Lobon, as they have helped me grow in faith and leadership as I serve others.

I would also like to acknowledge Beth Kalbac for introducing me to Claudio Perez, the CEO of Agape Jail Ministries in South Florida. Beth was touched by my angel story and encouraged me to do the mission work I am currently doing in See Horse Miami.

Last but not least, I would like to acknowledge Mike O'Donnell and his now deceased father Robert O'Donnell for their support and encouragement to help me start See Horse. I am very grateful to Bob for donating the funds to purchase a pony and pay his expenses for the first year. The pony has touched the hearts of the women and children who have been through the See Horse program by helping them find hope and purpose.

INTRODUCTION

This story is told through two different sets of eyes. First are my eyes, my experiences. The stories chronicled in this book were created during the time I was in a coma. As I lay in a coma seemingly unconscious and unaware, I was miraculously processing the events surrounding my life-saving healthcare. These events manifested themselves in the form of dreams. They were a mixture of current events peppered with decided and unresolved issues in my life. These dreams became my reality. I truly believe that while in my coma, I was a part of another dimension in time. Could it have been the Afterlife?

The second set of eyes belongs to Howard Rankin, who spent more than thirty years as a clinical psychologist and researcher, listening to peoples' stories. Subsequently, as a writer with a strong interest and expertise in the science of how the mind works, Howard now brings meaning to peoples' personal narratives in his work as an author.

1

My Life

Barbara

I had been blessed in living the dream life with privilege and unique opportunities. Being at the peak of my career, working as an architectural rendering artist for some of the most prominent architectural firms, defined me as a person and an artist. Through my notable career, meeting people of influence and affluence made me aware that I had come a long way since growing up in the small town of Mitchell, Ontario, Canada. My son Chris, born in Vienna, Austria during a five-year work stint in the early nineties, was now a fifteen-year-old teenager.

Over the decades, striving to be the best that I could be in my profession sometimes left me feeling empty. It seemed the harder I worked, the more I made, the more I spent, and the harder I would have to work to pay for it. I was on the hamster treadmill of life. Being very fit and healthy, competing in reining events with my Quarter Horse, and, most importantly, raising my son Chris brought me immense joy. But still, something seemed amiss.

I sensed that without some kind of balance in my life, I was surely working my way into an early grave. Feeling this pressure made me question my very existence. Maybe there was something greater than me. But what?

Though still loving the tropical climate and all that south Florida had to offer, in 2008, I was swept off my feet by a handsome, heroic, well-built, all-American firefighter named Mike. There was the promise that this true family man with two lovely daughters would give Chris and I the completeness of a family. As the relationship blossomed and our families became blended, our roots became grounded in Miami. Adjusting to our new life certainly came with its challenges, but we loved each other and were willing to make the sacrifices and compromises necessary to work through our issues.

As the 2009 spring rolled in, the biggest issue we faced was fear of the deadly H1N1 flu virus. We were especially nervous as both of Mike's daughters embarked on a five-day cruise. Floridians were on high alert. Anytime a student was diagnosed with flu virus, the school would be closed and fumigated until deemed safe for the students to return. This flu was frightening. Both the young and old were dropping like flies.

The week before Mike's hunting trip in November, I came down with what seemed to be the common flu. I contacted my mother after a terrifying nightmare where the Grim Reaper appeared beside my bed watching me as I lay dying. Frightened by what I told her, she immediately placed me on her church group prayer list. My boyfriend had become very concerned about my health and had a lot of apprehension about leaving me in this state. He even suggested that he would cancel his trip, but I assured him I would be just fine. I think he had the sixth sense, because he was adamant about me seeing a doctor and requesting Tamiflu.

I was showing no signs of recovery, and on Wednesday, November 11th, my son, who was home from school because of Veterans Day, was able to drive me to the doctor. My physician said I had bronchitis and loaded me up with prescriptions. The following day I felt worse, and by Saturday, I was a mess. As I woke up that morning anticipating Mike's arrival from his hunting trip, I was short of breath and had to wake my son Chris. He tried to comfort me, but I was getting worse. By 9:30 a.m., he called 911. They were there in minutes, and after checking my vitals, they dismissed any concerns. This assured me I was fine and potentially over-reacting. I decided to take a shower and start my day. A rendering had to be completed by late afternoon to make my deadline. There was no time to waste on being sick.

I can recall a moment of weightlessness as I exited the shower before finding myself on the floor. My son was in the next room and overheard the commotion, and quickly rushed to my side. He immediately called 911 again even though, out of embarrassment, I begged him not to call. A different crew of paramedics arrived in minutes. With my blood sugar way over 300, one of the crewmembers, a friend and colleague of Mike's, insisted on taking me to the hospital.

Still conscious, I could hear the sirens blaring. I lay motionless in a state of surrender, still believing that this was all highly unnecessary. I felt as if my body was spontaneously combusting like a cartoon character, and I began vomiting. Feeling helpless, I wished for Mike by my side. Losing oxygen to the brain in my hypoxic state, I soon lost all consciousness and from this point forward have no memory of what took place.

My son Chris remembers that day well. He met his friend after I was admitted to the hospital. Chris reassured him I was doing okay, and they left the hospital and drove to a nearby Mexican joint. Chris hadn't eaten since I had collapsed in the bathroom.

He wasn't too worried about me, as it felt impossible to him that anything seriously bad could happen to me. In the middle of a conversation about guacamole, his cell phone rang with "Momma Morello" showing up in the caller ID. He picked up eagerly to see if everything was okay and was surprised to hear the nurse. "Come back soon," she said, "your mother misses you."

Within five minutes, Chris was back at the hospital. He walked through the sliding glass doors to the security counter.

"I'm here for Barbara Morello, she's in room 36," he said to the uniformed guard.

While the man looked up the information, all Chris could think about was how long he would have to wait in the uncomfortably small waiting room until I was released.

"There's no Barbara Morello in room 36," the guard answered. He paused, "Are you talking about the Miss Morello in room 47?" Chris shrugged and replied, "Yeah, sure, whatever, that's it."

He buzzed Chris through, who slowly walked down a long hallway, looking hesitantly at the rooms lining his left and right.

"Forty-four, forty-five, forty-six," he whispered to himself as he approached room forty-seven.

He couldn't believe he was in the right place. This room was much larger than the rest and filled with the constant, ominous sounds of machinery beeping and whirring. There were several nurses bustling around the bed in the center. *What's going on?* Chris thought. A nurse opened the door, interrupting his confusion. "Are you Christopher...?" Her voice faded as he got a glimpse of the scene unfolding. A redheaded woman lay in bed, connected to several machines that made her look small and weak. The ventilator breathing for her made her look like a doll— delicate and pale. Chris was shocked; he couldn't recognize the figure lying in front of him. Then the realization came, washing over him like a wave breaking onto shore. This was his mom.

A short time later, I was in the dark unknown, as an evaporated person in a mysterious and frightening place.

A coma.

2

FIGHTING FOR SURVIVAL

Barbara

Prelude to the Coma Dream

On this first day in the hospital, doctors were making an attempt to stabilize my heartbeat. A normal beating rate for adults is between 60-100 times per minute; my heart was racing at 150 beats per minute, which put me in tachycardia, and at risk for a stroke. The doctor had a conversation with Mike about this perilous situation, and they decided it would be best to cardiovert my racing rhythm. This is a procedure that uses electricity to shock the heart back into a normal rhythm.

In addition to the cardioversion, I was intubated and put on a ventilator. Whenever my condition changed for the worse, it sounded an alarm. The melody of the alarm reminded me of a Mexican truck horn, or the car horn from the TV show The Dukes of Hazzard.

The room was very cold, which caused me to feel chilled. The ventilator tube made my mouth dry, suppressing my tongue and irritating my throat. These things contributed to my constant discomfort, setting the stage for my coma dream. I wasn't aware of what was happening, but my subconscious was processing everything that was going on around me and doing what it does best: trying to make sense of it all. I was on the edge of death and needed my heart to be shocked to sustain my life. Somewhere in my brain, it registered that I needed electricity or I would die.

Coma Dream

I was being pulled in several directions, but I couldn't tell you what directions those were. My sense of self had completely evaporated. Everything was jumbled and absurd. From somewhere came a thought: *This must be what a ghost feels like. Am I asleep? Am I dead? Where the hell am I? Am I in hell?*

The distant rumble of thunder echoed through my distorted perception of time and place. I looked down at what I thought were my feet splashing through puddles as the wind and rain pulled me—whatever me was—aimlessly down the street. Recognizing nothing, I realized I didn't know where I was or even what year I was in.

My tongue felt like a block of wood, heavy, stiff, and dry. I tried to swallow, but my throat was just as parched as my tongue. It was as if sandpaper had replaced the lining of my mouth, leaving me desperate for water. The feeling of dehydration was overwhelming; all I could think of was my need for relief. But my confusion about my current state kept me from coming up with anything rational. My mind drifted between thoughts of thirst and bewilderment as I tried to figure out where I was.

Then, through the storm, I heard the faint voices of two men speaking. They spoke with urgency and seemed desperate as the first voice yelled "We need to shock her heart or she'll die!" The situation seemed dire. I wanted to believe they were talking about someone else, but there was something foreboding about the tone of his voice that made me feel very anxious. I could feel my heart; it was pumping blood through my body with an unusual rhythm of distress.

"Could they be talking about me?" I wondered. Intuitively, I knew they were.

Clutching my trembling legs, I curled my body into a fetal position desperately attempting to regain clarity and avoid the truth. Still dry-mouthed and unable to swallow, the feeling of pending mortality haunted me.

The faint voices of the men faded away as the bizarre sound of a beeping horn began to assault my ears. I didn't recognize it immediately but it reminded me of the truck horns I heard in Mexico. Where had the voices gone? Did they leave without helping me? Who was going to shock my heart now?

The absence of the voices forced me to assume the worst. I needed to find a way to get my heart shocked in order to survive. There was no time to waste. I had to find electricity.

I heard the Mexican truck horn melody again and found myself behind the wheel of a pick-up truck driving down a four-lane highway in New Mexico. White-knuckled, my hands clung to the wheel as I sped down the road in search for something that could be used to harness enough electricity to keep me alive. Off in the distance, there was smoke rising from the interstate. *Ah, an accident. Maybe there is something useable from this?* I thought. *Something. Just let there be something with power.*

The mysterious sound of the truck horn was becoming irritating, but I couldn't tell where it was coming from. It played continuously in the background, adding to my mounting anxiety. Suddenly the meaning of life seemed so volatile; it was out of my control. Taking it for granted was no longer my automatic pilot. Approaching the accident scene with great anticipation, I prayed that God would deliver.

In my delusional state, I believed the salvage laws in New Mexico stated any person of lawful age had the right to repossess a wrecked vehicle if they were the first person to inquire, providing the driver of the wrecked vehicle was charged with a DUI. If I was the first person to ask, I could be granted the rights of ownership for the vehicle. Using the engine parts like a generator, its power could be harnessed to create electricity. It seemed like a plan.

Approaching vehicles in the eastbound lanes were backed up for miles. Dark, thick smoke from the burning wreck painted a scene of doom against the greenish sky. Ahead, I could make out the silhouetted form of a truck and trailer nose down in the ditch, and a state trooper waving the rubberneckers on. It seemed to take forever to reach him.

As I approached the scene of the accident, I lowered my window. The officer frantically gestured to me to keep driving.

"Officer, could you please tell me if this wrecked truck and trailer belonged to a drunk driver?"

"Ma'am, please, keep moving."

"But sir, I need to know."

Impatiently, the state trooper leaned in to my open window and said in a reluctant tone, "Yes, ma'am."

"Am I the first to inquire?"

He nodded impatiently.

"Please, officer, I need the registration, insurance, and license of the drunk driver in order to be granted the rights to the vehicle to save my own life." My eyes now focused on my watch, implying there was no time to waste.

"Well, ma'am," he grumbled in a raspy southern drawl, "I don't know about this one. The owner of the truck and trailer comes from influence. This is no slam dunk. You'll have to find an attorney to be able to repossess the woman's truck and trailer. Her daddy is a big wig in this state."

"Sir, you don't understand," I cried. "I need it now, or I'll die. Please can't you just overlook standard procedure this one time?"

"I'll go get the papers," he grumbled, "but you'll have to present it to an attorney." As he gazed at me like I was already a corpse, his tone suggested he wanted to assist but was uncertain whether this accident would actually help my cause.

With apprehension, I waited for the officer to retrieve the documentation from the wrecked truck and trailer. The toxic gray smoke traced an outline of his oversized body as he trudged back over to my vehicle. His weathered hand emerged through the window, waving the papers in my face as he muttered, "Good luck with this one, ma'am. It won't be easy. At the next exit, get off and head north for about a quarter mile, and you will see an old red brick building where you'll find the New Mexico Attorney's office."

"Thank you!" The truck lurched forward as my hand forced the gear into drive. I could feel my sick body traveling down the highway of death.

Hoping an attorney was still there, I pulled up to a historic red brick office building. Trusting the state trooper's directions were correct, I grabbed the first parking spot. The building was absent of life. It was just after 4:00 p.m. and most businesses had closed for the day.

Fear began to overwhelm my ability to think as my faculties were slipping away.

This can't be it. I'm too young to die, I thought while approaching the entrance of the office building. Picking up the pace, I marched through the entry into the foyer and down the hallway, skimming the signs on the doors. Finally, halfway down the hall, I saw a black sign with raised brushed nickel letters: "The New Mexico Attorney's Office."

Pulling the heavy glass door open, I stepped in and strutted toward his desk, extending my hand and introduced myself. "Hi, I'm Barb Morello."

"What can I do for you?" the young attorney asked as he stood and shook my hand. His disinterested gaze boasted arrogance, and his greeting lacked enthusiasm.

I placed the papers on his desk and got right to the point.

"I found a wrecked vehicle with a drunk driver, and I need to shock my heart," I said with urgency. "I understood if I came to this law firm, I could be granted the rights to this truck and trailer." Before I even finished my sentence, he began checking the files. I couldn't let his intrusive behavior stop my dialogue, so I continued. "Using the truck and trailer, I should be able to generate enough electricity to shock my heart, and that'll keep me alive."

"Miss Morello, I'm sorry to inform you," he said with a smirk, "But I see in my files here, uh, I see who the drunk driver is. The woman belongs to a very prominent family here in New Mexico. Oil family and uh, well we're not going to be able to help you, Miss Morello, with this situation. I suggest you find electricity somewhere else."

I detected no empathy.

"Please, no!" I pleaded. "I don't know where to go to find it. Now what am I going to do? I'm going to die if I don't have electricity!" I wailed hopelessly while slouching down into the chair, clasping the arm rests as if they would be the last things I would ever hold. I could not understand how this woman's truck and trailer took precedence over my life. *Just because she was from some well-established family with good connections, I end up the loser,* I thought while leaving his office.

Defeated, I climbed back into my truck and left the premises. With a heavy, bewildered heart, I woefully rolled down the road to find the interstate exit.

Howard

The Worldly

As I watched Barbara's experience unfold, I wondered what was going on. Truck horns, lawyers, accidents, and electricity…what was this all about? Perhaps Barbara's narrative was just some random associations that lead one from another to create a confusing mass of sensory impressions that have no organization or meaning. However, the brain is a storyteller that doesn't like confusion. Eventually, I came up with an interpretation.

Like many of the other experiences that follow, this sequence seems to be a combination of reaction to sensory input from the activities going on around her and associations with past experience.

The ventilator alarm was making a sound that reminded Barbara of a Mexican truck horn. The concept of Mexico triggered a thought of New Mexico, where Barbara knew the environment could be hostile and changeable: very hot during the day and cold at night. It is quite possible that Barbara's body temperature was changing pretty dramatically as her body went through various traumas and procedures.

Barbara's brain had stored several associations with power in the form of electricity. She vividly remembers visiting Niagara Falls as a young girl and being overwhelmed by the magnitude of the falling water and how that power was turned into electricity. The power of those falls was majestic, awesome, immense, and yet terrifying. The water was transformed into incredible energy, but now, she only needed a very small amount, a drip of the falls. Any more would kill her.

These associations, triggered by the events in her hospital room, fashioned the story.

It's not just the symbolism of a narrative that is important, but also the emotion. In this sequence, Barbara was motivated by an intense desperation to get electricity.

In addition, there is the beginning of a constant theme: the lack of social and political power. The attorney tells her that she cannot have the rights to the truck, because the driver is the daughter of someone who is well-connected. By implication, Barbara cannot be saved because she doesn't have a higher worldly standing. In her hour of need, Barbara is turned away. She begins her quest for power and ultimately finds it in a different form.

Barbara's upbringing is relevant here. Her father had all the power in the family and was the ruling authority, and she, like everyone else in her family, was at his mercy with no apparent recourse; a narrative of anger and helplessness. He gave his skills and power to other people and never recognized his children's talents and accomplishments. Around her father Barb was often terrified and helpless—two of the themes in this experience. As Barb admits, she learned to never question authority and

21

passively and regretfully accept her fate. Maybe that was about to change.

As Barbara lay in her bed, literally on the edge of death, her quest for electricity was about her search for the life force, which came from the heart and had the potential to empower and transform her entire body and mind. In some ways, Barbara's experience was about a re-birth, and even though she wasn't aware of it, she was about to manifest her life story through the narrative sequences that occurred over the next two weeks. Her narratives would not only reflect her life story; they would also take her in a fundamentally new direction. It's almost as if her life themes and conflicts were not just revealed in her coma, but resolved there, too. Soon she would find a different sort of power.

The book relates ten chronological events that occurred from the beginning of Barbara's coma. It's unclear exactly when they started. Barbara did her best to reconstruct the events by dictating them into a digital recorder immediately after being released from the hospital. That was when her sister Carla was able to make the connection between the stories that were forming in Barbara's mind and what was happening all around her as she lay apparently non-responsive in her hospital bed.

The dreams that Barbara was experiencing were actually triggered by daily occurrences and interactions with loved ones and the medical staff, and through tastes, touch, smell, conversations, crying, and other sensations. Her coma is therefore a window into the workings of the mind. Stripped of rational consciousness and communication with the outside world, Barbara was trapped in a bubble constructed by her stories—like the rest of us. Our stories might be informed by some higher conscious

22

functioning, but the roots of our thinking and reality are laid bare by Barbara's experience. The American psychologist William James called the unconscious emotional connections and associations that lurk in our psyche "the fringe of consciousness." This fringe is vague but weaves the narratives of our mind that directs our lives. Through association and memory, outside stimuli create a chain of associations that we have to construct into a coherent story. We are led down an associative highway that, if we are not careful, creates our reality. Perception is a reality defined by this automatic connection of ideas and emotions, a process that is often beyond conscious control, especially if you are in a coma—and even if you aren't. The combination of past experiences, present sensory stimulation, and the emotions thus created will combine to form a story that is at the heart of a meaningful and transformational experience.

Amongst the ten Coma Dreams are two encounters that have redefined Barbara's life. These are mind-blowing in themselves, but also ultimately mind knowing; they tell us a lot about faith, narratives, life and death, and how, in the unlikeliest of circumstances, we can resolve those mysterious conflicts that threaten us. When she emerged from the coma, Barbara discovered that she had undergone some incredible changes physically, psychologically, and spiritually. She exchanged a secular worldview for a spiritual one. In the end, for me, Barbara's experience is both the story of a miracle and the miracle of the story. You decide for yourself.

The Spiritual

My first Coma Dream, "Quest for Electricity," was about finding electricity to shock my heart. I was troubled because this challenge brought about a desperate search to find a greater power. In my mind, it was to be in the form of electricity. Indeed, my subconscious knew to look for a higher power, but how tragic that I looked for man-made power and not the spiritual source of the almighty power found in God. In my mind, I believed all I had to do was find truck parts like an engine that could be used as a generator.

Self-sufficiency often leads to making poor choices when we rely on just our own strength and understanding.

Paul says, "For when I am weak then I am strong." I realize this sounds like an oxymoron, but the deep meaning is about surrendering to our ways so God can work in our lives. But he said to me, "My grace is sufficient for you, for my power is made perfect in weakness." (2 Corinthians 12:9 NIV)

The phrase "Let go and let God" sums it up. That doesn't mean we sit on our butt and twiddle our thumbs. We are taught from childhood to solve our own problems because no one will do it for us. The contradiction in this narrative is that it is not exactly the truth. But how could we possibly know that? We are not born knowing God. We normally only find Him when we hit rock bottom or we're faced with illness or death.

Most of us come to God as a last resort because we realize we have exhausted every resource. The solution is always found in prayer and surrendering our will to God so He can help us work it out according to His will for our lives.

The other disappointment that left me feeling desperate and devastated was that my life seemed to have lesser value than someone "coming from influence." This was demonstrated in the coma dream when the attorney said he could not help my case because the woman in question came from a powerful family. This is a big problem in the world we live in, as too many times people with power get preferential treatment that can lead to corruption. When we put our trust and understanding in ourselves and others, we are ultimately let down. God always has the perfect plan and the power to execute our wants, needs, and desires.

King Solomon said, "Trust in the LORD with all your heart and lean not on your own understanding; In all your ways acknowledge Him, And He shall direct your paths." (Proverbs 3:5-6 NKJV)

This does not encourage us to be irrational, but rather to embrace faith and seek God in times of trouble. Adversity is merely God's design to draw us closer to Himself.

Where do you seek answers for your problems?

3

CARIBOU ELECTRIC

Barbara

Prelude to the Coma Dream

On this day, I was placed into a CAT scan, which may have alerted my senses that I was in a cave. Because the scan made loud electrical noises, it may have triggered my brain to believe it was electrical current surging through my body, as described in this chapter. There was a phone constantly ringing in this dream sequence. I learned at a later date there is a phone constantly ringing in the CAT/MRI room at that hospital.

After hearing the bad news from my CAT scan, Mike and Carla discussed that I could be a vegetable or, at the very least, blind. My sister cried uncontrollably, and it may have been what triggered my brain to believe it was crying from the howling huskies or the wailing woman described in this dream sequence.

The ventilator continued to sound an alarm, which became increasingly annoying. In addition, I could still feel the dryness in my mouth and inability to swallow because of the air being forced into my lungs through the endotracheal tube lodged in my throat.

Compression inflating cuffs (guarding against DVT's; deep veir thrombosis) were wrapped around my lower legs, causing me distress.

I felt very cold and damp, uncomfortable and restless.

Coma Dream

After such a disheartening meeting with the attorney, my foo exploded onto the accelerator and the truck sped off. The dimming light accentuated the leafless trees as dark-robec ghosts pointing the way. Following their cue, my heart seemed to skip a beat. In the rearview mirror, I saw the desolate terrain fade out of sight.

Ahead, there was a new form of life emerging against the billowy yellowish clouds. With arms that stretched out and suspended atop towering skeletal structures, the power lines resembled alien beings. From their glass insulators, tensed wire spanned from structure to structure sizzling and crackling with high voltage. It was a sign that could not be ignored.

My eyes followed the power lines until they vanished into the horizon "That's it, that's all I have to do," I muttered to myself, "I just have to follow them until they terminate at a substation."

The sun was lurking just above the horizon and casting long, dancing shadows of purplish-grey. The air felt cool as darkness began to settle in for the night. *I still have time*, I thought, while glancing at the clock on my

27

dashboard.

I resumed my pursuit of electricity. My body felt sluggish, restless, and without a spark, but my truck sped down the highway full throttle in the fading light. My mouth felt like it was lined with dusty old chalk. Swallowing was not an option; it felt like there were stones weighing down the muscles in my throat.

The chill of the night air began to feel uncomfortably cold. The heater failed to blast warm air. It felt like I was driving in an icebox; there was simply no way of warming up as the cool air stuck to every surface in the truck.

I could see the faint outline of mountains off to the right. The Mexican truck horn continued to play in the background but was now gently lulling me to sleep. But my determination to save my life powered my faculties.

"Come on, Barb, you need to stay awake." I shook my head to regain vigilance while making my way down the deserted four-lane highway.

I don't know how it came to be, but just like that, I went from New Mexico to driving down a highway in Alaska. Then I was hit by the sudden realization that I had to find a pack of Huskies. It shouldn't have been a problem, as I was now in Alaska. Almost as soon as I thought it, I noticed a blur of movement in the trees to my right. The blur became clearer, and I could pick out pairs of legs and a streaming tail. It wasn't a pack of huskies, but a lone husky.

As he drew nearer to the side of the road, it suddenly became very clear to me: the dog could trade his life for mine. All I had to do was run him over and I would have the opportunity to live. I would be granted the chance to be harnessed to electricity at a substation. It appeared that fate had turned in my favor, as the animal decided to run in my direction. He jumped over the guardrail and, as if he knew his purpose, ran right into the front of my truck. There was a heavy thud followed by a jolt, and my truck absorbed the impact. The sound of cracking glass and crumpling metal caused every muscle in my body to tense up into a ball of agony. My eyes closed momentarily as fresh blood splattered on to the broken windshield. It took every ounce of strength to keep my thoughts from spiraling out of control. With my foot now pressed firmly on the brake, I wheeled over to the side of the road and jumped out to survey the aftermath.

It was painless for the dog. With a speed of at least 60 miles per hour, he had been cleanly run over. He was dead.

A tear rolled down my cheek, followed by a steady stream. "What have I done?" I cried out. "Why does saving my life have to include a sacrifice so agonizing? How badly do I want to live?" The sensation of sorrow brought back traumatic memories. I suddenly felt the same anguish and despair that I experienced when my beloved childhood dog, Mustard, was hit by a truck. Mustard had always reminded me of a Husky. His was the first death that I faced as a child; I don't think I ever got over it. I grieved for him like no other.

What if this dog has an owner? I thought. *They will be devastated when they learn the fate of their prized possession.* I hated the thought of causing even more pain.

29

There wasn't enough time to waste thinking about the Husky, so I trudged back into the damaged truck and sputtered off down the road. Judging the distance through the faded light, I could almost see the end of the metal structures carrying the high voltage electricity. *Less than a mile, I thought,* trying to encourage myself.

As I approached my destination, a sign caught my attention. "Caribou Electric Sub Station," I read as the headlights illuminated the letters. I pulled over, paused, and took a deep breath. This was it. The entryway of the building looked worn, as if it hadn't seen employees in weeks. I stumbled out of the truck, landing in a ditch hidden by the overgrown foliage. Nature had clearly begun to reclaim her territory. The tall grass moved and swayed as if to pounce on its next victim as I navigated the rugged path. The long weeds wrapped around my ankles, forcing me to pause and free myself from their grasp. Glancing back, I realized the truck was no longer in view.

Would I be able to find my way back to the truck?

It was scary out here and there didn't seem to be any people around for miles. Anything could happen to me and it would stay a secret. I could disappear and no one would know where to look; or worse, I could die from heart failure and no one would find my body.

I pushed those thoughts out of my mind and pressed onward, even as the damp, cold air sent me into uncontrollable shivers. With only minutes left of twilight, I had to keep moving. The overhead wires hissed and groaned, while coyotes howled in a foreboding rhythm. It was unlike any sound I had ever heard before. Everything about the noise seemed strange,

30

eerie, and ominous.

I struggled to walk with frigid bones and shortness of breath. The rhythm of my heart beat harder with each step. I was so discouraged and exhausted, the last fifty yards to the substation seemed to take an eternity. Then, there it was. A small concrete building enclosed within a ten-foot high galvanized aluminum fence. Barbed wire sat proudly atop the perimeter of the fence, intimidating unwelcome visitors.

I slipped through a narrow opening and made my way one step at a time to the entrance door. The sizzling, crackling wires overhead taunted and overloaded my senses with both fear and elation. The place was desolate; there were no signs of life. I would just have to wait here and hope an employee would show up in the morning.

"How much worse can this get?" I wondered. I needed to find a place to lie down and sleep. It was dark now, and the only source of light came from a small lamp mounted to the outside of the doorway. It glared down stark and unflattering, casting unsightly shadows from the metal casing.

With my stiff, cold hand poised on the door handle, I gently squeezed and turned the knob. The door seemed to open on its own free will, as if possessed by supernatural forces. It slowly lured me in.

I cautiously stepped over the threshold into the gloomy, dimly-lit room. After my eyes adjusted to the darkness, a false sense of bravery motivated my adventurous spirit to explore the room for a makeshift bed. My face was chilled to a pale blue color, and my hands stiffened as though rigor mortis had already set in. Looking down at the concrete floor, I knew

31

the loneliness would drive me to madness. The thought sent an icy draft straight up my spine.

Shivering, I gazed into the cramped space. My eyes narrowed and strained as I made out the shape of a cot placed near the wall. Every step forward raised a cloud of dust that glimmered in the dim light. It would have been beautiful if it didn't cause me to choke. Sweeping away years of old dusty cobwebs, I grabbed the cot and shook it, freeing it from its layer of dust.

There I was; alone in an abandoned substation, lying on a filthy cot as my life ticked away, with nobody.

My thoughts were interrupted by the sound of a ringing phone. "That's odd," I murmured. After struggling to free myself from the cot, I followed the ringing sound to a corner in the room.

"Hello? Hello?" I yelled into the receiver.

"Why did you do it?" screamed a man's voice on the other end.

"Do what?" I retorted.

"Kill the husky!" he shouted angrily.

"I didn't have a choice. It was my life or the husky's."

"I can't console my wife," he screamed. "Listen…"

All I could hear was a hysterical woman wailing at the top of her lungs. It sounded like she had just lost the love of her life. She gave the phone back to her furious husband.

"What have you done?" he continued. "The other dogs are also crying for their lost companion. Listen to this…" He held the receiver out again, and this time, all I could hear were dogs howling for their lost brother.

"These dogs are our livelihood," he sobbed. "Who is going to compensate me for my loss? These dogs work for a living. We are simple people of simple means. We live in a cave. Our home is a carved-out space from the side of the rocky hill." As he ranted, I wondered how he knew it was me who had accidently killed his dog.

I could hardly stand it. His wife and their other huskies were crying like they were all sentenced to the electric chair. *What's wrong with this picture?* I thought, *What about my life? Does anybody care about whether I live or die?*

All night long, the phone continued to ring. Every time I answered, it would be the same thing: the man's wife crying followed by the howling huskies. The night seemed to last forever. My guilt was overwhelming; I felt terrible for his wife and their loss. What made me think that my life was that valuable? Why bother? *I should just let myself slip away,* I thought. After all, nobody was crying over me or even cared about where I was.

The morning light trickled in through the cracks of the door, illuminating the space with hope. I had made it through another night. As I lay in my cot, wondering if and when somebody would walk through that door, I caught a whisper of noise. My ears strained to pick up more sounds as I struggled to free myself from the deep impression of the canvas fabric.

The sound of grass crunching and snapping under the weight of footsteps in the crisp morning air became louder with each step toward the entrance. The rusty doorknob squealed in protest as it was turned

33

by the unknown presence approaching me. The door was slowly pushed open, and a man in uniform peered inside.

"Good morning, Miss Morello."

The voice was reassuring, but how did he know my name?

"Let's get this done," he said, while pointing at the door.

He looked handsome in his Caribou Electric uniform. *Here to rescue a damsel in distress,* I thought.

"What took you so long?" I asked, trudging toward the door. He did not answer my question; he just guided me out.

"Okay, Miss Morello. This is a very expensive and dangerous procedure that we're about to do. The voltage we are using is deadly if not in the perfect dosage. You must stand on this downed power line for three seconds only. If you stand on it one second longer, you will be killed. So you need to count to three, then step off the line."

He demonstrated the method, counting to three as he looked at me solemnly.

"I need you to sign this waiver saying we are not responsible if anything goes wrong. You need to sign here and give me your billing address. Expect an invoice within thirty days for $5,000. Don't worry if you can't pay it at one time; installments can be arranged."

I wondered why he couldn't just control the amount of power himself. Why did I have to be in charge of my own fate?

"That's a lot of money," I said. He didn't bat an eyelid or make a comment.

"Okay, Miss Morello, I'm going to stand over here and pull the lever which will allow the power to flow through the line. Do exactly what I told you."

Taking a deep breath, possibly my last, I maneuvered my body and feet into place. *Will I feel pain?* I wondered as he placed his right hand on the lever.

"Remember, count to three, then step off," he said in a tone that registered no concern over whether I lived or died. One swift motion of his arm was followed by the sound of a transformer purring in sync with voltage coursing through my frail body. Shaking violently, I counted "One, two, three." Then I stepped off the line, just as he instructed. Despite violent shaking from the ordeal, I knew I was safe.

In a detached voice, he said, "Miss Morello, that was great. You are going to be just fine. Caribou Electric will send the bill to your Miami address."

"That was a lot of work to save my own life," I muttered.

Howard

The Worldly

The significance of this sequence lies in Barbara's perception of the value of her life. There is also the possibility of the idea of a heart transplant playing in this dream, as she says, "Why does saving my life have to include a sacrifice so agonizing?" Does someone or some thing have to die so she can be saved?

At one point in this dream sequence, her story focuses around someone who lives in a cave. Maybe the thought of being in a cold cave and the feeling of isolation placed her in the state of Alaska, the last frontier. Or perhaps being in a cave is a metaphor for living outside of the material world.

The choice of Husky that needed to be killed eventually resonated with Barb when I asked her about her own experiences with dogs. That's when she told me about her first experience of death with her own dog, Mustard, who resembled a Husky. It happened when Barbara was twelve; she was devastated and grieved for a long while.

But why did she have to kill a dog? Why did she have to experience so much guilt? The answer came quickly.

When Barbara was twelve, her parents went on a two-week vacation to Switzerland. Mustard stayed at her father's factory instead of staying in the family home. The night before her parents were due home, a voice in her head told her to pick up Mustard from the factory. Barbara, not wanting to be bothered then, made the decision to pick him up in the morning. Even though she continued to hear this voice in her head, she didn't act on it. She convinced herself that he would be fine overnight.

The following morning, Barbara went to her dad's factory, which was a short five-minute walk from her house. Upon arriving, she did not see her beloved pet where he had been chained to the post that supported the overhead sawdust collector. Her dad noticed her and walked over with a very grim look on his face. He announced the bad news; Mustard had been crushed that very morning by the   truck that loaded up the sawdust.

36

The dream could be a resolution of the guilt that Barbara had carried for three decades. The wailing woman in the dream could have been her.

This sequence is also about personal value. Barbara told me that there were times in her childhood when she wondered whether her authoritarian father cared whether she was alive or dead. The conflict is that Barbara wants to be saved, but her concern is that saving her life has costs, and in any event, does anyone care enough? Is she worth it? On one hand, she is caught in a desperate need for love and validation, and on the other hand questions whether she is worthy of them.

In the end, the debate is resolved by the dispassionate substation manager, who simply puts the number of $5000 as the amount needed to save Barb's life.

It's no surprise that having been saved, Barbara expected the Caribou Electricity bill to arrive for six months after she woke up from the coma despite her rational mind knowing that it made no sense. At some level in her psyche, there was still a need to pay for being saved.

Barbara

The Spiritual

In this coma dream, believing that the life force of power was man made in the form of electricity, the revelation that I needed a sacrifice in order to live occurred to me. At that moment, a blood sacrifice materialized in the form of a lone husky. The husky seemed to know his purpose; that he would surrender his life for my survival, just as Jesus knew His purpose was to shed His blood for humanity. In the Old Testament, animals without blemish were used to atone for the sins of God's people. Then God sent His only son to make atonement for our sins, that we may have eternal life.

God presented Christ as a sacrifice of atonement, through the shedding of his blood; to be received by faith. He did this to demonstrate his righteousness, because in his forbearance he had left the sins committed beforehand unpunished. (Romans 3:25 NIV)

I wondered why the guy at the electric substation couldn't just control the amount of power himself. Why did I have to be in charge of my own fate? We are all in charge of our own fate when it comes to what kind of power we seek. The power that is acquired through money, esteem, and material wealth is derived from a worldly perspective, which is powered by the prince of this world, Satan. He is the opposite of love but has us convinced that he is the only source of love. The love of money, greed, influence, beauty, and material wealth is temporal. It is short-term in this life and leads to darkness in the next. This type of power comes from darkness.

I finally found the man-made form of power, but it came at a cost, physically, monetarily, and spiritually. The challenge was to stand on the downed power line for exactly three seconds or death was inevitable. What kind of challenge is that? What if I didn't count the timing of 1-2-3 perfectly? What if I didn't have the funds to pay the bill? What if I died? I definitely needed to be plugged in, but to what power source? The real source of power does not come at a price. Jesus already paid the price and is free to anyone who takes Him as their savior—and this power is eternal not temporary.

"For God so loved the world that he gave his one and only Son, that whoever believes in Him shall not perish but have eternal life." (John 3:16 NIV)

While the manmade source of power initially provided a temporary source of life-giving sustenance, I was still in a dilemma.

Will you consider whether you have ever personally received Christ by faith as your Lord, King, and Savior?

4

SECRET LOTTERY NUMBERS

Barbara

Prelude to the Coma Dream

The notes from this day informed me that some good friends visited—a couple I met at a 2008 Landmark Education forum. They had met each other years earlier at a racetrack. She worked as a cashier and he placed bets on the horses. They eventually married after dating for several years; he was fifteen years older than her and well-off. These facts play out in a very bizarre way in my coma dream.

Because they were in their retirement years, they were discussing ways of generating more income. He was in the process of resurrecting his retired concrete construction company, and I had been helping them in this venture by producing architectural renderings. There was the promise that I would be well compensated if this business took off. I suspect this is what triggered the coma dream sequence. Trying to arouse and encourage my entrepreneurial spirit, she painted a success story, hoping that would bring me out of the coma. She is depicted as visually unflattering in this coma dream, but in reality, she is an attractive redhead.

Coma Dream

The voice was raspy. It was the kind of mature voice that commanded authority. Was it the wisdom and experience that resonated with me? Or was it the underlying tone of manipulation that alerted my senses? I couldn't put my finger on it, and it made me feel anxious. When I looked in the direction of the voice, I saw nothing.

A chill crept up my spine. A figure emerged into the dimly-lit room. With trembling hands, I tried to maneuver my body to a sitting position. I was just too vulnerable reclining. I blinked to readjust my vision, but nothing changed. A flash of movement in my peripheral vision ignited my adrenaline. I only caught a glimpse of a dark figure moving toward me and it spiked all my senses.

An aromatic scent drifted through the room, bringing with it a brief moment of tranquility. It reminded me of those therapeutic perfumes made with essential oils. However, its calming effect gave way quickly to tension as the figure came into view. It moved with a choppy, uneven gait, wobbling over until it was only a few feet away. The horror etched in my face and soul could not have been mistaken.

It was a woman. She had a protruding brow that shadowed her dark eyes, giving her a harsh appearance. Her eyes were large and bulged outward; wrinkles lined her face, adding years to her image. Short, curly hair in a dull auburn color framed her face in an unflattering style.

"I am the mayor of Coral Gables," she boldly declared. "I'm here to help you out so we can make lots of money together. You are strong and you can fight this. You just need to get better. And I can help."

I was taken aback by her generous offer of making money together. It was a proposal I couldn't refuse.

Tired of being stuck in this dimly-lit room and the limitation that restricted me, I looked down at the cold stone floor. I could see my own breath, and the temperature seemed to keep dropping. There was no relief for my unquenchable thirst and anxious state. Discomfort plagued my entire body. I felt as if I'd been buried alive, trapped in a coffin deep under the earth and forgotten. Hopelessness, loneliness, and restlessness had become my norm. I wondered how I could escape this place. Could this woman of influence and power actually bring me out of this situation? Could she lead me to the promised land? Could she help me make money? I wanted to believe it. I just wanted out of here. Could she be my savior? I was ready and willing. "Just tell me how," I pleaded.

In the background, I could hear footsteps approaching us. A man spoke with an endearing and confident tone. His voice seemed to command respect, until she spoke to him. Then it was clear who was in control.

He was attentive to both the woman and me; I could tell by his mannerisms that he cared about her, yet he spoke affectionately to me as well. Did he know me? Somehow, his voice was familiar.

He took my hand and said, "We're here for you, baby. Don't worry we're going to get you out of this thing. You just need to get well." He laid my hand back down and left the cold, dark room just as quickly as he had come.

I was alone with the mayor again. She was the only person who seemed to possess the power to save me. I was hopeful.

"Okay, Barbara," she said encouragingly, "I have the secret lottery numbers that have entitled me to money and power. And if you can guess them, I'll pass them on to you. And when you have them, your health will be restored and you will be wealthier than you could ever imagine. I'm not allowed to tell you what the numbers are, but I'll stop you when you guess the correct combination. I've been the mayor in this town ever since having these lucky numbers, and I get whatever I want. As a young woman, I slept with an older gentleman who passed the secret numbers on to me. That's how I've maintained my power and fortune. Nobody knows this secret, but I'm willing to let you be the next person to hold the special numbers. You can never give them out or you will lose your power. Now start guessing."

"478," I said with enthusiasm.

"No, that's not it," she said abruptly.

"261?"

"No."

"2123?"

"No"

"2122?"

"No, not yet."

"2120?"

"Nada."

"2125?"

"No. Sorry, Barb, not even close."

"5, 10, 20?"

"No, keep guessing," she cheered me on.

"31, 40?"

"No," she said in an exhausted tone.

Seconds became minutes, which turned into hours, which seemed like days. I was beyond frustrated; there was no end to the guessing. Exhaustion began to reclaim my mind. My thoughts were spiraling out of control. It seemed that no amount of guessing could be successful. But I still didn't give up. It was as if I had been wandering in the desert for days in a delirious state, looking for water, and someone had given me hope of a spring. The will to survive is the strongest of all instincts, so I continued guessing.

"1, 2, 3, 4?"

"No"

"1, 2—I don't know!" I shouted. "Why can't you just give me the numbers?"

"You must guess them."

"Why does my survival seem to come at a price?" I cried out.

Howard

The Worldly

On the surface, this might seem like an obvious extension of Barbara' real-life involvement with her friends from Florida. The couple seemed to have the key to money and power, and they could therefore possibly help Barbara escape the trap she was in. But what was the trap? Was it the coma? Or was it something else?

While it is tempting to assume that the trap was the coma, it could be something more significant. Is this dream once again about the core issues in Barbara's life: identity and value? As we shall see more and more Barbara's relationship with her father consisted of her desperately seeking approval and never getting it. As a result, Barbara held many self-doubts about her value as a person and as a woman.

So, here comes a woman with power. She has the answers. But how did she get the answers? She got the secret to success by attracting a man who had the answers. Now, the mayor was clearly in charge and in control. It is, however, only worldly power.

No matter how hard Barbara tried, she couldn't get the answers. This is also a familiar echo from childhood. She never could do enough to get approval, even with schoolwork. The emphasis was on what she didn' know, not what she did. Barbara was the child who could bring home an A and be questioned on why it wasn't an A-plus. It made her feel that she was never quite good enough, and she never got any solutions as to how to get it right. Her inability to guess the right numbers in this sequence could be a reflection of her confusion as to what she needed to do not just to succeed, but be valued as a person. Or, it could be that she was looking for worldly answers to spiritual questions. And, as we shall see, that theme continues.

Barbara

The Spiritual

I was thirsting for water, which spiritually reveals I was searching for answers. The story where Jesus meets the thirsty woman at high noon by the well and offers her a drink of water comes to mind. To quench her spiritual thirst, the Lord first confessed the truth about plain H^2O: "Everyone who drinks this water will be thirsty again." (John 4:13 NIV) Then Jesus made a bold promise: "Whoever drinks the water I give him will never thirst." (John 4:14 NIV)

In one sentence, he shifted from everyday life to everlasting life.

I was not looking to Jesus for answers, but instead to a woman of influence with special lottery numbers, who claimed to hold the secrets to its transfer. Convinced there was no other way, I was more than happy to give it a shot. However, it seemed like an eternity passed as I tried to guess the correct lottery number combination, which only ended in despair.

This dream sequence holds significant value. Is this not what we all do in life? We put our faith in others who hold high positions and who claim to possess the keys to success. No matter how hard I tried, there was no success in relying on my own strength. The real secret lies in knowing and relying on the strength of our Savior Jesus Christ.

We truly gamble with our lives daily when we do not know Him. We never know when we'll be faced with death, and for believers, absence from the body means presence with the Lord.

Non-believers will find themselves in a place of eternal darkness. Do you really want to gamble with your eternal life? Heaven or hell—you don't have to gamble on this. Eternity is eternity.

What unmet expectations have left you thirsty or unsatisfied?

5

RECORD RING DEATH

Barbara

Prelude to the Coma Dream

Notes from this day showed that the compression inflating cuffs that were designed to prevent Deep Vein Thrombosis (DVT), a condition that occurs when blood clots form deep in the body, became very tight around my legs. This was probably due to the extra seventy-five pounds of liquid weight that my body gained from being on life support.

It was noted that I was very restless, thrashing and fighting to free myself from the cuffs, causing the nurses to restrain me.

There was a discussion in my room between the medical staff and my family members about the deadly H1N1 virus, and how it causes organ failure by depleting oxygen exchange to the vital organs.

I must have overheard this discussion because coincidence or not, that's how the death played out in my subconscious world. The inflatable cuffs tightening and releasing pressure on my ankles created the illusion of a snake-like thing (represented by the record rings) wrapping around my lower legs. Physical touch or pressure plays a major role in how my subconscious interpreted the stimulus. When I had my lungs suctioned or taken off the respirator to see if I could breathe on my own, the sensation of not being able to inhale oxygen also played into this dream sequence.

My mother was by my side the whole day. She was very distraught and probably voiced the view that it might be better for me to die than live in a severely disabled, vegetative state, which was still a possibility at that time.

Coma Dream

I found myself back in 1979, one of the most vulnerable times of my life, in the small town of Mitchell, where I grew up. There was a man in this town who believed he possessed wisdom granted by a higher power. He was smug and never quite cared for me much. He thought I was wicked and led by my own desires; according to him, I was one of Satan's own. He could never prove it, but he would tell convincing stories about my self-centered nature to anyone who would listen.

He prided himself on being right and was determined to prove he was. After all, he was a righteous Christian who lived his life by his own strict interpretations of the Bible. Unfortunately, my mother was one of the people that listened to his judgmental beliefs. He wanted to expose what he thought was the truth about me: that I would do anything to be the most

49

beautiful woman, even if it meant jeopardizing my life.

"If you are willing to go along with it, I have a way to prove it," he told my mom.

Mom was a Christian and just loved the Lord. She never missed Sunday church; it was her way of recharging her batteries for the week. Nor did she ever miss any church functions, fundraisers, or socials. The church was her life. If anyone could prove there was a misfit unworthy of the Lord's mercy, she was willing to listen, even if it meant listening to a plot to rid the world of impure people, like me.

She loved me, but she hated sinners.

This man was convinced that any association with a sinner would send him to Hell. So, he revealed a plot to my mother that would expose my weakness. He told my mom where to buy a record called *How to be a Barbie Doll*, which was a hypnosis audio on how to become the world's most beautiful woman in twenty-four hours. It had already been banned in the United States due to the suspicious deaths of its listeners. It appeared as if listening to the record was directly linked to the murders of several young women, although they were still under investigation.

Mom debated whether she should purchase the audio program. She loved me but was persuaded by the man's arguments that, if I were worthy and pure, I would not be tempted by the message. However, if I did choose to listen, I would surely deserve the consequences that followed. After all, I knew that death was a possibility. He didn't think he was trying to kill me, at least, not directly. He thought my inability to resist temptation would lead to my demise; so, whatever happened to me would be my own fault. He wouldn't feel guilty for my death, and there would be one less sinner for him to worry about.

My mom purchased the record.

After sending the package to me by mail, she began to have some regrets. She was worried, but it was too late to retrieve it now. Had she done the right thing? Maybe she should have raised me with more faith or a better understanding of sin's repercussions. Or maybe she shouldn't have listened to him. But the ball was in motion, the record was on its way, and the only thing she could do now was to pray for me to make the right decision.

It was my first year studying interior design at Fanshawe College in London, Ontario. I was insecure and felt ugly compared to the other girls. Growing up in Mitchell didn't do much to promote self-esteem. People in a small town don't like to see anyone get ahead or stand out. They had ways of putting you in your place.

I was delighted when I received a package, and even more excited when I read the title: *How to be a Barbie Doll. What a wonderful gift from my mom!* I thought. I studied the packaging, reveling in the notion of becoming irresistible.

As I pulled the record out of its jacket, I noticed a warning label but didn't want to take the time to read it. I was more interested in what the album cover said. Holding it in my hands, I studied the image of the most beautiful woman I had ever seen. She had the features of a Barbie doll: tall, blonde, and blue-eyed; everything about her screamed perfection. "And to think, I could look like her," I marveled.

The anticipation was killing me. The description read as follows:

"How to be a beautiful and desirable woman that all men will want. By listening to the whole album, your mind and body will transform into that of an attractive woman, as seen on the album cover. Your hair will grow long and your skin will rejuvenate, giving you a more youthful appearance. Your lips will become full and sexy; your bone structure will alter, giving the appearance of high cheekbones and a well-defined jaw. As your bone structure goes through metamorphosis, your eyes will become larger with beautiful long lashes, and your waistline will taper down to eighteen inches. Your breasts will grow larger and more upright. Your hips will take on a sexy shape, while your legs will become longer, sleeker, and more well-defined, accentuating your new, fuller butt. Next to transform will be your attitude. You will notice that with your new look, you will become conceited and arrogant—perfect for attracting men; they all want what they can't have."

How could my mom possibly know to give me this gift? I thought while placing the record on the turntable. The warning label located in the middle of the record glared at me. I still chose to ignore it, even though it boasted the hazard symbol of a skull and cross-bones. *How lethal could the record really be?* I thought, scrambling to set the needle in its correct position on this vinyl promise.

"Caution, do not start the hypnosis recording unless the warning label has been read. By starting the record, your fate has been sealed. There is no stopping it once you have set it in motion. The record has now taken on a life of its own. You cannot run or hide. Death is inevitable. The rings on the record will start to unwind and wrap around your ankles. They will continue to wrap around your leg until the entire subliminal message has played. They will constrict your blood flow by cutting off your circulation, depriving oxygen to the rest of your body until you lay lifeless. This entire process is slow and agonizing. It should take a full twenty-four hours for the subliminal message to be played in its entirety."

"What have I done?" I screamed.

A long snake, black and shiny, slithered toward me. Its movement was intentional, as if it had radar that tracked my every movement.

I darted for the door. The deadbolt snapped shut, trapping me in the room. My trembling hand clasped the handle, but the door was immoveable. I was cornered.

Panicking, I jumped onto my bed and tried to use my uncooperative sheets as protection. But it was too late. The black snake-like thing slithered onto the bed and began striking at my ankles, like a reptile securing its prey. I could see the vinyl record getting smaller as the black lines unwound and morphed into the snake that was wrapping itself around me.

Surely, this was hell! In my agony and terror, all I could do was wait and gnash my teeth desperately. The tension only increased as the vinyl rings pulled tighter and tighter around my legs. Then, there was a low hissing voice that sent a chill straight to my bones. I couldn' understand its message, but knew it was something evil and satanic.

"Is this some kind of sick joke?" I screeched. "Someone get this thing off of me! Get it off! Get it off!" I began kicking and flailing again, in the hope that I could escape my suffocating vinyl prison. My panicked body harnessed every ounce of adrenaline that it could manifest, but the rings never loosened their grip. I realized I was in for an exhausting, drawn-out death, thrashing and struggling to the very end.

"Someone help! Help me! It's cutting off my circulation! Please, please help me! Help!" But my yelling was in vain; I knew no one could hear my screams.

I didn't give up easily. I continued to struggle and pull against the snake that ensnared me for hours. Throughout the night and into the next day, I tried to free myself. By the time I came to the end of the twenty-four-hour recording, I was exhausted. I could feel deep bruising and lacerations where the rings cut into my skin. My muscles burned from thrashing for so many hours and my lungs gasped for breath from the constant exertion. I knew I was dying; there was nothing left in my body. I was spent; there was no extra spark of energy in my limbs and no hope left in my thoughts.

I could feel my oxygen flow lessen slowly, agonizingly. Every breath I took seemed to do less and less until it became futile. It was as if the air supply had been emptied and I was being forced to hold my breath. Still gasping desperately for air, I could feel whatever life was left in me draining away. Exhausted, oxygen-depleted, and succumbing to death, I heard my last breath slowly hiss out with an eerie rattle as both lungs

54

collapsed.

The Worldly

This dream has many of the elements of Barbara's struggle.

There is a male figure espousing similar attitudes and beliefs as her father. He wants to give Barbara a morality test to see if she will pass.

Again, we have the theme of Barbara having to prove herself. She is being given a very definite test. Then her mother, although uncertain, is persuaded to go along with it. In this sequence, Barbara's mother had some doubts and regrets after sending the potentially deadly audio recording, but by then it was too late. There's also a sense of hypocrisy: a self-righteous man trying to give a woman a morality test that will be very difficult to pass.

The theme is, again, the battle between the spiritual and the material. The subject of the audio recording once again is the desire to be beautiful, wanted, and loved. There are some things you should know about Barbara's teenage years. She summed it up well when she described it like this:

"I didn't feel attractive at the best of times, so when my so-called best friends ridiculed my appearance, I was devastated. In my heart, I longed to look pretty and wear makeup, but I submitted to their disapproving opinions. How was I ever going to attract a guy looking as I did? I felt betrayed by my friendships and rejected by the boys I liked because of my androgynous appearance. I had no boobs, short blonde hair, and blue eyes with spaced front teeth. I developed a complex about my appearance that led me to feel inferior."

So, it's not difficult to see why Barbara, like so many girls, "reveled" in the prospect of becoming physically irresistible. But there was also a downside. This wasn't just about becoming beautiful; it was about the ability to resist temptation.

Barbara's description of her recognition of temptation but unwillingness to really consider the consequences of her behavior is a classic description of the human predicament. Who hasn't pursued a dangerous action, knowing that it was foolhardy but choosing not to focus on the risks anyway? In this case, the warnings were all too clear, but still Barbara chose to ignore them. The risks are always very clear in hindsight.

The record unravels only to become a snake determined to kill Barbara. The symbolism of the snake is inevitable and foreshadows things to come. A slow, agonizing death squeezes the life out of Barbara.

Her mother has been an unwitting accomplice to her daughter's death. Barbara failed the test and paid for it with her life. She opted for the worldly over the spiritual.

As Barbara and I discussed this sequence further, she made a connection with the vinyl rings of the record with the rings of trees. Tree rings are a record of the tree's growth. Each ring is a record of the tree's journey and its history. The rings that wrapped Barbara in a death grip took a full twenty-four hours to unravel. Was that the unraveling of Barbara's existence, the record pun   definitely intended—of her life and choices? Was the unfolding vinyl record really her life choice coming to get her? We all have to account for our choices, and they can come back to bite us at any time, but especially when standing at the gate of eternity.

Barbara

The Spiritual

"Record Ring Death" is an illustrative metaphor for life flashing before our eyes, exposing the poor choices with their consequences that we have made along the way. The warning label on the record is symbolic of the warnings in the bible that Jesus talks about when it comes to sin' repercussions. In this sequence, I relished the notion that I could be the most beautiful woman in the world that could have any man. Without realizing it, I was trying to become an idol. God's first commandment is "You shall not have any other gods before me." (Exodus 20:3 NIV) Also "for the wages of sin is death, but the gift of God is eternal life in Christ Jesus our Lord." (Romans 6:23 NIV)

What was I thinking? Knowing it came at the price of death displayed by the skull and cross-bone symbol on the record label, I still continued to set the needle in motion. I am embarrassed to admit this and be transparent in this book, but on careful examination of what we view on TV— *American Idol*, *The Bachelorette*, *The House Wives of wherever*, even Walt Disney's *Cinderella*—there is an illusion that women must be beautiful to get the man of their dreams and live happily ever after. We are programmed from childhood to be   the best and the most beautiful

57

and to have all the attributes that attract our prince in shining armor. Again, was this about a rescue attempt for a damsel in distress, or was I really living out my desire for perfection to be admired and wanted? Either way, it's not pretty. By chasing after my desire to be perfect, beautiful, and sexy, the record rings ended up claiming my life.

The question is, aren't we all in some way or another trying to be the best, have wealth and power, be beautiful, and have status—often at the expense of others and ourselves? Social media facilitates our desire to be noticed and adored by our fans and friends. We spend hours daily boasting, bragging, and showing off our selfies and pictures that flatter us beyond reality.

How can we want something so bad that it leads to dying? Chasing after selfish ambitions directs us to making poor choices, for one, and secondly, we can become so consumed with our own desires that we overlook how we affect others. In Matthew 3 and John 6, Jesus talks about the consequence of lusting after our own flesh and working for things that don't last. "Do not work for food that spoils, but for food that endures to eternal life," Jesus says.

How many of us are consumed with social media? Has it replaced the need for Jesus in your life? Does it rule your life and jeopardize relationships with others? Do you get satisfaction out of the sheer number of friends and fans that follow your accomplishments? If the answer is yes, you can understand how easy it is to get swept away with selfish ambitions and pride, which lead to idolatry. "Where you spend your time is where your heart is," Jesus said. How much time do you spend in prayer with Jesus or in relationships with loved ones?

The third tragedy of this coma dream comes when I realize I set my fate in motion, and there is nothing I can do to alter its course or save myself. It makes me aware of all of us living a life of not accepting Jesus or spending time doing things with no eternal value, and realizing in death that it's too late—ending up in hell, fire, misery, and darkness, and saying "If only I listened to those who tried to share the importance of being in a relationship with Jesus." It's like the story about Lazarus and the rich man in Luke 16:19-31. This is an account of a very rich man who lived a life o extreme luxury. Lazarus laid outside the gate of this extremely rich man's home, hoping even for a scrap of food, and was completely passed over by this uncompassionate rich man. Eventually, they both died, but Lazarus went to heaven and the rich man went to hell. Appealing to Father Abraham in heaven, the rich man requested that Lazarus be sent to cool the rich man's tongue with a drop of water to lessen his agony in the fire. The rich man also asked Abraham to send Lazarus back to earth to warn his five brothers to repent so they would never join him in hell. Both requests were denied. Abraham told the rich man that if his brothers didn' believe the scripture, neither would they believe the messenger, even if he came straight from heaven.

"Do not be amazed at this, for a time is coming when all who are in their graves will hear His voice and come out—those who have done what is good will rise to live, and those who have done what is evil will rise to be condemned." (John 5:28-29 NIV)

"Enter through the narrow gate. For wide is the gate and broad is the oad that leads to destruction, and many enter through it," (Matthew 7:13 NIV)

If that doesn't scare you, nothing will. "The narrow gate" means the gate to heaven, which, apparently, is not easy to get through.

Hell is very real. It was created for all the angels who fell from heaven. It was not meant for mankind. But if man or woman is disobedient and chooses to live a life with no regard to what Jesus came to liberate us from (sin), then he/she will end up there too.

Do you know where you are going when you die? Who or what are your idols?

6

FOUND DEAD IN A DUMPSTER

Barbara

Prelude to the Coma Dream

On this day, the medical notes suggested that I was still very restless and again needed to be restrained.

The tube that was carrying away my waste smelled particularly bad and some strong coffee grounds were placed next to my bed to try to mask the odor. This may have contributed to the association of being in a garbage dumpster.

The TV was on most of the time, with local news playing regularly. This could have been what triggered my subconscious mind to create the channel 10 news broadcast.

I was still in the inflatable cuffs, and they continued to feel very restrictive.

Accounts from my family tell that there was a constant bedside vigil as my mother and loved ones diligently prayed for me while there was talk of ulling the plug.

Coma Dream

The stench of decay brought me to consciousness like smelling salts to a boxer. I could see my body lying in a dumpster, contorted and twisted like a discarded rag doll. The dew formed by the humid morning air had coated my corpse in a fresh blanket of moisture. There was an old, drunk, homeless man sleeping next to my body in the garbage.

"I'm dead. I'm really dead." I shuddered at seeing my cold, damp, rigid body lying like a slab of meat on a butcher's block.

I was stunned as I surveyed my blue-tinted corpse. I realized how surprisingly effortless it was to transition from one state to the other.

But why was my body lying next to a homeless drunk? Was he using me as a cushion, or was he too inebriated to notice that death was propping up his head? I couldn't tell if I was more alarmed by the out-of-body experience or at seeing myself lying in a dumpster next to this man.

How had this happened? Why hasn't anyone discovered this ghastly scene yet? I thought as questions continued to race through my mind.

I tried to push this intruder off my body, but my hands passed right through him. I tried again and again before giving up, realizing I no longer had any physical ability in this world.

My thoughts circled back as I began to feel pity for myself. I felt a deep concern for my lost dignity. How embarrassing to be found dead in garbage; people walking by would think I was a prostitute who overdosed. What were my family and friends going to think when they saw this? I wasn't alive to defend myself. They were going to think the worst. My life was just as empty and valueless as this old, drunk, homeless man, contributing nothing to society. This was the legacy I would leave behind, a wasted life of self-destruction caused by my own poor choices.

"How do I alert the police?" I wondered, as I felt a strong urge to do something productive. Then, I remembered that I was useless in this current state, nothing more than a ghostly audience to life. I would have to wait for someone to discover my body.

There was a yawn as the old man stretched and placed his hand on my cold corpse. "Aw. Ew. What the...?" he grumbled, slowly retracting his arm in a clumsy movement. Finally waking up, his gaze fixed on what he had just touched, and he screeched. There was a flurry of movement as he awkwardly shoved my body away, using his thin, stiff legs in a useless effort to escape. "Ahh!" he shrieked. Panicked by the sight of death, he began screaming for help, piquing the curiosity of some passersby. They strolled over, ready to have fun with this crazy old man's paranoia.

Black vinyl string was slung over the side of the dumpster, along with other rotted debris. As the people peered in over the filthy metal edge, their eyes followed the string from where it draped to the coiled mess wrapped tightly around my ankles. The drunk continued to thrash about

63

trying to free himself from the rotten garbage and my corpse.

"What's going on?" asked one of the guys. His eyes widened and his breath quickened when the scene registered. "Quick, go flag down a cop!"

Stunned by what they had witnessed, the group scrambled in different directions, as though they were guilty of a heinous crime.

Flashing blue lights from the approaching police car gave me a sense of relief. It was only a matter of time now before my family would discover that the Barbie Doll Recordings had claimed my life.

Mixed emotions coursed through my jumbled thinking. What was worse, the family I loved doubting and testing me, or the fact that I was now dead? How could I tell this tragic story, and who would care? *But I was too young to die; it's just so unfair,* I thought.

Another cruiser pulled up just minutes after the Channel 10 news team arrived. Yellow crime scene tape was stretched around the perimeter of the dumpster.

"Give me your full name," demanded the attending officer to the homeless man.

"Ah, yeah. Ah…" was all the poor drunk could manage.

"This guy is not making any sense," the cop snickered. "Hey, lieutenant, you got some leftover coffee in the car? We need to give this guy a shot of something."

"What about this one over here?" the officer said. "What's her story? Do you think the old man bound her legs with black string, had his way with her, then killed her?"

Hacks, I thought, watching the two men discuss the possible motives and theories behind my mysterious death. They didn't seem to have the slightest bit of empathy for me. Didn't they have daughters? Couldn't they see how tragic this was?

The dumpster was illuminated in cruel detail by surreal rays as dawn broke over the buildings. This disturbing scene would be forever etched in my soul. It wouldn't be long before the Channel 10 news would be reporting this mysterious story. The air seemed heavier than usual that morning.

"This is Channel 10's Jessica Simons reporting live this morning from downtown Kitchener-Waterloo's industrial area. Police are saying a body was discovered early this morning in a dumpster next to an elderly homeless man. It appears to be another senseless casualty from the Barbie Doll subliminal recordings. Black vinyl string was found wrapped tightly around the ankles and legs of this young college student, who attended Fanshawe College in London, Ontario."

"How did she end up here in Kitchener-Waterloo, in a dumpster? Police have been trying to eradicate these recordings, which have been responsible for claiming the lives of many young college girls. An investigation will be launched to find out who was responsible for giving Miss Morello the deadly record ring recordings."

The Worldly

This dream speaks for itself. Barbara has finally crossed a line. She has ended up dead in the garbage next to a homeless alcoholic. It would be hard to imagine anything more demeaning than that. Moreover, she is there by her "own poor choices." Of course, Barb learned from her childhood that it's always her fault. Everything is her fault.

The question of who gave Barbara the recordings is left open to investigation but, of course, we know it was her mother at the urging of someone who symbolically represented her father. The policemen who show up to investigate the scene are just two more men who don't understand and have no compassion. They also assume a sexual connotation; the old man has tied Barbara up and "had his way with her." Is the sexual lens the only one through which men look at Barbara? Are these worldly horrors the result of poor spiritual choices?

Barbara's desperate and demeaning fate is also going to be broadcast to the world when Channel 10 News shows up. More shame and humiliation.

Barbara has gone beyond rock bottom. Where can she possibly go from here?

The Spiritual

This coma dream is a tragic representation of a life with no eternal value. My life was lived running after false values and fool's gold, which ironically ends up taking my physical life, but also claims my spiritual life. That's dying twice. The second death occurs when Jesus comes back in the second coming. That's when judgment is made on every human being living or deceased. He will open the Book of Life, and if your name is not written in it, your fate is sealed and punishment will follow. The second death will be more frightening than the first.

"Anyone whose name who was not found written in the book of life was thrown into the lake of fire." (Revelation 20:15 NIV)

Should we be worried? I don't know about you, but I do not want to be thrown in a lake of fire. That's enough to scare me into making sure my name is written in the Book of Life.

How do you spend your life? Are you prepared for eternity?

7

FUNERAL PREP

Barbara

Prelude to the Coma Dream

The notes revealed that the medical staff had turned off my ventilator to see if I could start breathing on my own. I couldn't. In this coma dream, I must have interpreted not being able to breathe as someone shutting the power off.

There were more tests and procedures involving noisy dialysis and CAT scan machines. I believe my brain conjured up the scenario that I was in a textile factory, probably due to the noise generated from the hospital machines. Because I was in the scanner, I could sense the cold, hard, metal surface, which may have contributed to my believing I was placed on a cold metal table for funeral preparations.

My sister Carla, a paramedic and part-time floral designer, was my advocate at the hospital, and tried to fix me up a little that day. She brushed my hair, plucked my eyebrows, and put moisturizer on my lips. I had so much hair that the nurse asked that it be kept tidy or they would

have to shave my head. My sister knew how much I loved my long, thick
beautiful hair and worked diligently to keep it tangle-free and braided.
Because flower arrangements were brought to my room, Carla may have
been indicating placement locations for them. I believe my brain
processed her presence as a loved one appointed to take care of my
funeral and floral arrangements, as well as my appearance.

Coma Dream

I could hear the eerie whirring of sewing machines in the background, needles driving through fabric at high velocity in the old Kitchener textile factory where I lay. I was on the third floor, the only floor left where the historic building still had some life. I thought this must be the site chosen to prepare my body for the funeral after being found dead in the dumpster outside. It struck me as remarkably convenient, being so close to where I was found. What a great way to keep the cost down.

My attention drifted to my hair. There was so much of it, I thought, as I felt the gentle hands of a woman guide a brush through my thick mane. She was standing behind me, as my head lay on the end of the cold stainless-steel table. Her warm hands were comforting as she continued to tenderly stroke my hair. Somehow, she seemed familiar. Only a family member or lover could be as caring and gentle. The tone of her voice had such a reassuring quality. Then it came to me: it was my sister, Carla.

She's brushing my hair so I look nice at my funeral, I thought. She seemed so calm and relaxed, making me wonder if she knew how I died.

Did she hear the morning news and learn of my mysterious death? Did she know who gave me the fatal Barbie Doll recordings?

I was a corpse lying on a cold steel funeral prep table, unable to utter a word. How I wanted to speak to her! But how could I tell her that our own mother gave me the recordings? She was such a simple, God-fearing woman, whom I know really did love me. How tragic that my life was cut short. There was no second chance to redeem my sinful ways. *Pass Go, do not collect $200, and head straight to Hell,* I thought with a shudder.

I could hear my sister carrying on a conversation. Was it with me or someone else?

"I could place the flower arrangement here," she said. "Or would it look better over there?"

I knew Carla loved flowers and created stunning floral arrangements for weddings and funerals. Did she fly all the way down from Canada to help me look presentable at my funeral? I could feel her loving hands applying lipstick, as well as fussing over my eyebrows to make sure there were no stragglers. Thank God my sister loved me and cared enough to make me look pretty.

The humming of the antiquated textile machinery began to fade slowly into silence as the hustle and bustle of the room subsided. I wondered what the time was; could it be the end of the workday? I felt a sense of calm knowing that my funeral preparations were almost in order as the day came to a close.

"Okay, Barb, I'm going home for the night," came Carla's reassuring voice. Her footsteps moved toward the door, and she was gone. Following behind her were the footsteps of a heavier woman. My senses told me that she was an employee who worked in the textile factory, waiting for my sister to finish up. She, too, was going home for the night and was in the process of shutting down the power for each room.

There was an ominous snapping sound of a switch. *That's strange,* I thought, *Why can't I breathe?* There was no air to inhale and nothing to exhale; it was as if someone had shut off my personal air supply. Had shutting down the power to the factory also shut down my ability to breathe? How could that be? *Am I not even in control of my own breathing?* I wondered as panic set in.

"Somebody! Somebody, please come back! Come back and turn the power on! I can't breathe. Help! Help! I can't breathe!" I tried to shout but there was nothing I could do. No one could hear a dead woman. *That's it,* I thought, *I'm done.* Succumbing to death was my only option. Then it hit me: if I was experiencing gasping for air, then I must not be dead. *I'm alive!* I must not have died after all. My joy was cut short by another painful gasp for air; maybe this second death would be the final end. Then I heard another snap as the power switch was flipped back on. I felt the sweet sensation of oxygen entering my lungs as they began to rise and fall again.

Howard

The Worldly

In this story, Barbara feels love from her sister in the form of making Barbara look nice, albeit for her funeral. Even at this stage, life continues to be about her appearance. Even in death, Barbara feels the need to look good.

Two days before being admitted to the hospital, Barbara saw the Grim Reaper. Death was on her mind before her ordeal even began. In some ways, there is a certain appeal in death; the struggle for approval is over. In this sequence, there seems to be an acceptance of mortality, and even some peace until the discomfort of being unable to breathe is resurrected when the electricity is inadvertently turned off.

It is tempting to conclude that this is what happened, that the nurse flipped off the ventilator to see if she could breathe on her own. But perhaps that didn't happen at all. Perhaps the switch that was flipped was inside Barbara and not the one on the wall. Perhaps she decided she didn't want to die after all, and as soon as she felt that idea, she suddenly became aware of her breathing difficulty. What came first, the breathing difficulty or the desire to stay alive?

Barbara

The Spiritual

This dream is about regret—realizing I could have lived life differently by having a life rooted in Jesus. Being inflicted with the grief of being separated from my loved ones was unbearable, as life was just taken away and it seemed so final. When we live our lives according to scripture and in relationship with Jesus, we will see our loved ones again in Heaven and have no more pain and tears.

"He will wipe every tear from their eyes. There will be no more death or mourning or crying or pain, for the old order of things has passed away." (Revelation 21:4 NIV)

How can you live your life differently?

8

THE DEAL

Barbara

Prelude to the Coma Dream

I could feel the ventilator tubes in my throat, and they made me feel like a V-shape was cut out of my tongue. I also felt that there was something wrong with my left hand and arm—the result of a stroke experienced on life support.

Days before I was taken into the emergency room, I saw the Grim Reaper. I saw death. I called my mother immediately and told her of my foreboding vision. She was frightened by what I had shared with her, so she added me to her church's prayer list. Interestingly, I also had a vision of my stroke and shared that information with my son.

Coma Dream

I could feel the shape. A large triangular piece was missing from the tip to the mid-section of my tongue. *Who cut out the middle?* I wondered. It felt like the shape of a snake tongue. I pictured what my new smile would look like and shuddered at the thought. What a shock it would be for people to witness the smile of a serpent. Another terribl thought ran through my mind: how would I pronounce words with thi condition?

My hands lifted to cover my face in horror, and I realized somethin, else. My left hand wasn't reacting the same as my right; it was stiff and felt as if it were missing joints. I peered at it nervously and wa immediately mortified. My hand was clearly deformed, stuck in the shap of a lobster claw. All the joints in my fingers were frozen into a strang formation, rendering my hand useless. It was downright hideous.

I was uneasy and fearful at the thought of what life would be like whe I got out of this place, wherever it was. Feeling restless and restrained b my inability to leave this hell, I began to wonder if I would ever find m way back to familiarity.

Loneliness magnified my weakened state, making me feel stuck in cold and empty vacuum. I was powerless to control my ow circumstances. Being this helpless, I had no choice but to take whateve opportunity arose to escape this hellhole. "I'll just have to get through thi thing," I reassured myself.

Despair and depression began to crush any hope that remained, as tim became my enemy. Thinking of my deformity and hopelessnes swallowed me like the darkness that surrounded me. Minutes turned int hours, and hours seemed like an eternity in this gloom. It was as if th gates of Hell had opened up and swallowed me; nothing could reach m here, and nobody would ever find me. I was lost forever in the underbell of Hell. "Maybe I'm dead," I thought. "This must be what Hell is."

"There is a way," came an unexpected, monotonous voice. "I have been waiting for you."

As the mystery man leaned in to reveal himself, a dim light source emerged, illuminating him. Just one glimpse of him made me shudder. His nose was large and protruded from his face like a beak, creating unflattering shadows over his aged face. Large pores dotted his nose like craters, and his skin was weathered, reminding me of old, neglected leather. His blond hair was dirty and wiry and streaked with gray that poked out from under his dull brown hat. His mustard-colored trench coat only emphasized the gray undertone in his pale skin. A strange red glow seemed to emanate from around his neck. I thought that seemed a little peculiar. Was it a sign?

"I can help you," he continued. "I'm in the business of helping lost souls find their way home. However, it comes at a price, and my offer will expire in six minutes. First, let's assess the situation to determine the cost. Have you seen yourself lately?" he snorted. "Not pretty."

That's funny; I'd thought the same about his appearance.

"Look at you! You're a freak! Maybe a carnival would take you for their travelling freak show. Headlines could read, 'Woman with serpent's tongue and lobster claw hand performs tricks!' Can't you just see it now?" He laughed loudly at his own cruel joke. "That will be the only career choice left for you. Which brings us to the next question: how are you going to earn an income to support yourself and pay the hospital bills?"

"Well, I guess I never thought about that," I stammered.

"Let me be clear; no man is ever going to want you with those hospital bills. Who's going to pay those? They'll be in the millions. How come you don't have insurance? No man will ever want a woman with that kind of debt."

"Wow," I muttered, looking down at my mangled claw-like hand with tears rolling down my cheeks. Focusing momentarily on the split in my tongue, I realized he was right. Who would want me in this condition? I was a penniless, mangled mess.

"I don't have much to offer someone in such an unfortunate set of circumstances," he said with a forced smile, "But I do love you, so I'll make you a deal. If you will serve me for the rest of my life, I will take care of your hospital bills. I'm not a young man anymore, but I do have needs."

I paused for a moment, weighing out the pros and cons to the most important decision I would ever make. Handing your soul over requires serious contemplation. It was a great example of being stuck between a rock and a hard place; both options were terrible and the consequences for making the wrong choice were dreadful. Both choices seemed hopeless, so what was a girl in my situation to do?

I wondered how he could possibly love me, anyway. I didn't even know him, so how did he know me?

The dim light source cast a gruesome shadow from his predator posture, revealing deceptive intentions in his expression. I snapped my head around to examine his facial features more closely. Could he be Satan?

"My offer will expire in the next minute," he snapped impatiently. "You should consider yourself fortunate that I am willing to take you. The choice is rather simple; you don't have one. It's me or the grim unknown; which is looking tragic for you, young lady."

The pressure was on. My heart was pounding against my chest; my dry mouth rendered me unable to speak.

Is there any way for this to end well? I thought. I was being challenged with this choice and had no one to talk to about it. It would be such a relief to have someone to ask. Exasperated by my hopeless situation, I tried to put off the decision. Could he really provide an escape from this hellhole? Or was he tricking me into an even greater hell?

"Times a tickin'. It's now or never. Tick, tick, tick." He laughed harshly, taunting me with his sickening grin.

"Why do I have so little time to decide?" I shot back at him.

I had been alone with this dealmaker for all of six minutes and he was becoming increasingly pushy.

"I could walk away this instant," he retorted. "Then where would you be?"

All the difficulties of having to make it on my own raced through my mind as I studied the enlarged pores on his weathered face. The only reason I was still in this no-win conversation was my fear of being alone. My anxiety elevated as I stared into his eyes. They were an icy shade of

78

steel blue, but something else lurked in them. He had no emotions; emptiness radiated from his face as his true identity started to come into focus.

I could feel my will begin to waver as fear tightened its grip; this was not going to end well. I wanted to say no, but in such a weakened state my voice, in barely a whisper, muttered, "Yes. I'd better take the deal; I don't really have a choice here."

The large pores on his smug face tightened as the corners of his lips drew up into a sinister smile. "That's right, you don't really have a choice."

As he reached out his frosty, withered hand to touch my deformed claw-like arm, the reality of my choice hit me. I was selling my soul to the Devil. In that instant, the dim light source brightened and fully illuminated his face, revealing an expression of doom. He looked straight at me with ice in his eyes, burning a hole through to the back of my head. I could physically feel it, as if he had penetrated my skull with a dagger. I felt so defeated.

My jaw clenched in horror as I realized I was signing my life away as an enslaved prisoner. There was something in that moment of awareness that caused an intense reaction. Every ounce of my soul felt disgusted and violated. Surely God had created me for some other purpose, hadn't he? I couldn't go down like this. My mother always said, "Barbie, God created you to do His work." *That's it.*

A sudden jolt of defiance aroused my weakened mind and body, urging me into battle. I didn't know   where this burst of boldness came from, but I harnessed every bit of it. "Hell no! What am I doing?" I shrieked. "I take it back." I was on a roll now as the momentum carried me.

I hoped desperately that it wasn't too late to rearrange our agreement. "I'm not taking the deal. So, if that means I'll be a hideous, deformed mess stricken with loneliness and burdened with huge hospital bills, so be it! God has other plans for me. Away with you, Satan!" I shouted.

I had enough time to hear him mutter a curse as he spun around and vanished.

The feeling of death looming after me was frightening, but I didn't care at this point. I was going to die one way or the other, but at least it wouldn't be by the hand of the Devil.

I had teetered on the brink of temptation for what seemed like an eternity. I was about to dive into the abyss, but something stopped me; there was a part of me that just wouldn't go through with the deal. As I struggled, I sensed some force was helping me stand firm for my values and resist giving in to fear. I don't know where that strength came from, but I was simply glad I didn't do the deal.

Howard

The Worldly

The pivotal moment arrives and it is once again centered around Barbara's value as a woman and a person. The devil makes a pitch, and it seems like an infomercial. He summarizes her terrible plight, offers himself as the only realistic alternative, and puts Barbara under a time limit. I was half expecting him to offer her free shipping and a second deal absolutely free. These aren't merely marketing tactics; they are the tools of someone who knows how to hijack reason, and to suck you into the deal. Unfortunately, too much of advertising is an unethical effort designed to tempt you. It uses strategies lifted from social and cognitive psychology to persuade, tempt, and influence, even as it misrepresents or excludes facts and distorts reality. In a marketing society, the main form of communication is emotional manipulation.

The devil's premise is that Barbara will never be attractive or wanted by a man. Apart from her appearance, she has enormous debt; the devil knows which hot buttons to press. At first, Barbara agrees. However, she agrees by focusing on what she can't have rather than what the devil will give her. What is he offering? To take care of her, in return for her becoming a follower and satisfying his needs.

Satan's strong point is the notion that Barbara will always be alone and that seems to be the decisive factor. No one will ever want her.

Like so many people faced with seduction and a test of their willpower, Barbara knows in her heart that it is a bad idea.

However, there was something greater than fear that rose within her. It was hope. It was a belief that life was more than a beauty contest, that God had plans for her—a purpose and a value. Barbara was mystified; she didn't know where this force came from. It sprung unconsciously but resonated powerfully. For the first time, Barbara saw a different version of her life, one in which her value was divorced from her sexual value and worldly perceptions. Maybe for the first time, she stood up for herself and disputed the idea that her worth was only reflected in the approval of a man. After years of being challenged by men, she put her foot down.

A new narrative arose: "I have value in my own right, regardless of my appearance, regardless of my disabilities, and regardless of my financial situation. I am valuable. I have purpose."

The tide had turned.

Barbara

The Spiritual

"The Deal" demonstrates the spiritual warfare of Satan. In my critical hours, I truly believed my soul had left my body, which was sustained only by life support. This was the test of all tests. He knew my weakness and told me convincing lies of who I was, and what I would amount to. His tragic narrative left me feeling hopeless. When Satan convinces us we are without hope, he can really get to us. Through his deceptive influence and lies, I took the bait and agreed to his deal to sell my soul. Somehow, in the last second, my soul knew I had purpose and my default for a higher power (God) kicked in. I recanted the deal and an angel swiftly ushered me away.

What is your default?

9

VISIT WITH AN ANGEL

Barbara

Prelude to the Coma Dream

This is the one sequence where it is difficult to connect my experience to what was happening to me in reality.

The hospital notes suggested that I was still in serious discomfort, my heart continued to be on the edge of failing, and there was a serious possibility of needing a transplant. It was confirmed that I had sustained a stroke while on life support that could possibly leave me in a vegetative state.

After waking up from the coma, it was discovered that the stroke had affected my vision, causing visual disturbances as well as disruptions in my ability to process information.

Coma Dream

The calm voice—"You made the right choice"—came out of nowhere. "That was close. You almost made a deal with the Devil. He disguises himself well and tells very convincing lies."

And there he was. It was his eyes that struck me first—eyes that emitted light from the inside out and irises that were a vivid shade of sparkling turquoise. His presence was angelic; the light that radiated from his eyes gave him away as something not human. Despite the indisputable fact that he was a celestial presence, his manner and appearance were comforting and disarming. He wore a blue plaid shirt and denim jeans that appeared soft and worn. His skin was youthful and his expression bright; wavy, coffee-colored hair framed his face and formed a gentle mustache. He appeared to be in his early thirties, although I'm sure angels don't have ages.

"Take my hand," he said.

Immediately, despite my frail state, I reached out. I could instantly feel his warmth and love. The next thing I knew, we were flying to a destination that remained a mystery to me.

And just as suddenly as we began our flight, we landed. I found myself walking on old and worn cobblestone streets. The buildings reminded me of the historic architecture in European cities like Vienna. The familiarity of the city comforted me. We were not in Miami anymore.

The scene changed again and we were no longer on the streets. Mosaic tiles glimmered with hues of blue, green, and turquoise on the vaulted ceiling. Vivid shades of color shimmered like the crystal-clear waters of the Caribbean; brilliant hues shone like fine diamonds, dancing and reflecting their light on every surface. Some of the bigger tiles were set into gold inlay that glimmered into eye-catching shades of shiny, glittery rich color.

I have never been aware of colors like this before. It was like each hue emitted a radiant spectrum of colors. The acoustics, too, had a pristine quality all of its own, a whole new dimension of tone that I had never experienced before. It was as if sound had become three-dimensional. Inside this magnificent bathhouse, I could hear the sound of rushing water cascading, plunging, and converging into a pool of tranquil water. It was healing to my ears, healing to my soul.

Restful patterns in mosaic tiles adorned the bench that we sat on near the swirling water. Our backs rested against a wall boasting similarly exquisite patterns and shimmering turquoise hues that transitioned into the vaulted ceiling. Several grand ionic columns graced this space, inviting the senses to delight in its awesome splendor. Its sheer magnificence lulled my soul into complete submission as I receive God's healing.

The angel held my hand, radiating his love and warmth, and said, "Your body is too sick to inhabit. You can rest here awhile and enjoy the healing waters."

Finally, for the first time in   what seemed like an eternity of restless wandering, traumatic events, and apathetic people, something was different. Very different. Could it really have been the decision that I made at the last minute? Does Satan really disguise himself to convince you that he, and only he, can save you on your deathbed? *I almost fell for it*, I thought while soaking up the tranquility.

I was free. I didn't have to sell my soul. It made me shudder to think that I had been so close to resigning myself to eternity in Hell. Maybe everything I had experienced up until that point was like Hell: hopeless situations with apathetic people.

While we were sitting together, the angel said, "Barbara, it's not your time to go. We are sending you back to your body when it's more habitable. At the moment, you have the heart of a ninety-eight-year-old. However, we have blessed you with a healed heart."

I had known in my weak state there was something wrong. The struggle to move air in and out of my lungs was exhausting. The lump in my throat and pressure on my tongue was unnerving. But the feeling of dehydration was like getting lost in the desert without water, and not knowing when or if you would ever find a drink again. While in his presence, I did not feel any of these discomforts that had plagued me.

He softly squeezed my hand and turned so we were face to face. He looked deep into my eyes and I looked deep into his, noticing again the light emanating like sunrays.

He said, "Look at my eyes. I see differently, and so will you. When you wake up from your coma, you will see through different eyes. But do not be alarmed, as it's all part of the plan."

"Well then," I interjected, "what's my mission or the plan?"

"I do not know," he let me down gently. "I'm an angel. Only God knows that. I can tell you this; I am an angel of pediatrics."

"Then what are you doing with me?" I said, laughing.

"I was assigned to you because you will be working with children, and also giving birth to new life."

"Does that mean I will be having a baby at forty-eight years old?" asked.

He smiled. "It will be revealed as you go along."

I was confused. Baby? New life? Children? Angel of pediatrics? Seeing through different eyes? A healed heart? Waking up from a coma? What was going on?

Although I had many questions, I knew that what I needed now was relaxation and tranquility. It seemed like I had been terrified and on the run for such a long time, searching for ways to save my life. Now, the fear of my mortality had been lifted. God's grace has spared me. What could have been an everlasting life in Hell was replaced by the opportunity to live a new life. I was being sent back to fulfill a mission for God.

The Worldly

Interestingly, this is the one story where there are no obvious events in the hospital or memories that explain the associations, sensations, or thoughts that Barbara was having.

Barbara is transported across time by an angel to a special healing place. For the first time, she doesn't feel discomfort, even though the hospital notes suggest that she was still extremely physically agitated.

As she reviewed her life and felt free, maybe for the first time, she re-evaluated her story. "Maybe everything I experienced up until that point was like Hell: hopeless situations with apathetic people."

Maybe Barbara had based her view of her self, and to some extent life, on the jaded and false narratives of others. Maybe she was too rooted in the material world, where narcissism, money, and sexuality reign supreme.

The angel tells Barbara that her heart is healed and that she will see through different eyes, like him. But she is already seeing through different eyes; her perception of her self and life have changed.

The pediatric angel told Barbara that her mission had something to do with children. Was that literal, as in real children, or metaphorical, as in children of God? Barbara would find out in due course.

Regardless of the meaning of the message, Barbara's perception of her life and her mission had changed forever.

The Spiritual

In this dream, I was taken to the most magnificent place I had ever seen and made acutely aware that I was in a realm of spiritual healing and love. It's what happened next that completely changed my physical and spiritual life.

As my physical body lay dying in the hospital bed, my spirit was in the presence of Jesus, who called Himself the Pediatric Angel. Pediatric means "healer of children." We are all children of God. He granted me life by restoring my heart. I also experienced transformation of the heart in that I was reborn—spirit giving birth to spirit.

"Flesh gives birth to flesh, but the Spirit gives birth to spirit. You should not be surprised at my saying, 'you must be born again.'" (John 3:6-7 NIV)

I was told I would see through different eyes, as He did. Indeed, He was right. From the moment I came out of the coma, my physical vision was different, but my spiritual vision came into amazing clarity. His life transformative power has not only given me a second chance at life, but now know without a shadow of a doubt that I have eternal life in Heaven. will never have to experience that lonely dark hellhole that I experienced in my coma again.

"Very truly I tell you, whoever hears my word and believes Him who sent me has eternal life and will not be judged but has crossed over from death to life." (John 5:24 NIV)

One of the amazing things that I have learned is God does some of His best work while loved ones are incapacitated or in a coma. When believers are praying over the sick for healing and His protection, or when petitioning for their sins, God's work is amazing. Not only is this true for me, but I witnessed this through watching the healing that took place between my mother-in-law and her daughter. Inflicted with Alzheimer's and on her deathbed, not able to speak or make sense for some time, she uttered to her daughter in her last days, "I love you." After a strained relationship, the healing that took place on that day will live in her heart forever.

Ironically, the only way to save my own life was to die to myself by denying Satan's tempting deal. Our lives can only be saved through the precious blood of Jesus. We cannot save ourselves. Jesus often spoke to His disciples about the importance of taking up their own cross and following Him.

He made it clear by saying, "For whoever desires to save his life will lose it, but whoever will lose his life for My sake will find it." (Matthew 16:25 New Heart English Bible)

I often wonder: if I had not recanted the deal, where would I be?

My question to you is, "Do you know Jesus?" When we all meet Him on Judgment Day, He will ask, "Do I know you?"

"I never knew you."

"Not everyone who says to me, 'Lord, Lord,' will enter the kingdom of heaven, but only the one who does the will of my Father who is in heaven. Many will say to me on that day, 'Lord, Lord, did we not prophesy in your name and in your name drive out demons and in your name perform many miracles?' Then I will tell them plainly, 'I never knew you. Away from me, you evildoers!' (Matthew 7:21-25 NIV)

That simply means that you can claim to know Him, but does He know you? You can be assured He knows you when you ask for forgiveness of your sins and take Him as your savior. Also, I encourage you to find a bible-based church, join a bible study group, pray daily, and learn to rely on Him as you make Jesus the center of your life.

Jesus asks us the question, "What are you working for?"

Are we working merely to make a living and have a comfortable home? Can people ever feel satisfied, or do we always desire more? Do we need more to feel valued or do we need it to feel secure? If so, our Lord is saying that when you get all this you will find yourself wondering 'Is this all there is?' That is true of all humanity. The thing that makes human beings different from the animals is that having a full belly and a comfortable place to rest does not satisfy us.

To this hunger, Jesus said to them, "Then Jesus declared, "I am the bread of life. Whoever comes to me will never go hungry, and whoever believes in me will never be thirsty." (John 6:35 NIV)

Jesus recognizes the universal hunger for bread beyond physical bread. You cannot go anywhere on earth today without finding people hungry for something more than a full belly and a comfortable home. There is

91

restlessness about us that cries for more. Jesus recognized this. Everyone in this crowd wanted whatever it was He was offering. They did not understand what it was, but they wanted it. They sensed there was more to life than bread.

Through experiencing the fear of death, trying to save myself, feeling unworthy, experiencing an incredible restlessness, and feeling frightened, intensely sick, lost, physically deformed, as well as going through the process of death and being trapped in hell in these seven Coma Dreams, I can honestly say that it felt more real than living life. How can these Coma Dreams not make one search for the truth and experience transformation into a more Christ-like individual? It reminds me of *The Christmas Carol* by Charles Dickens. It's a story about a bitter old miser named Ebenezer Scrooge and his transformation into a gentler, kindlier man after visitations by the ghost of his former business partner and the Ghosts of Christmas Past, Present, and Yet to Come.

It is written in the Bible that those who have encountered death or Satan have been ministered to by angels. I love this verse in particular, which describes when Jesus was tempted by Satan in the wilderness:

"Jesus said to him, 'Away from me, Satan! For it is written: Worship the Lord your God, and serve him only.' Then the devil left him, and angels came and attended him." (Matthew 4:10-11 NIV)

Are you prepared to meet Jesus?

10

GOING HOME

Barbara

Prelude to the Coma Dream

From the notes and my family's record, it was my mom's last day visiting with me and she said, "Barbie, you are doing much better," which gave her the comfort to fly back home to Mitchell. Knowing on some level that my mom was returning home because of my progress probably created the notion that it was time for me to go home as well.

Mike, Carla, and Dino had been applying mouth and lip moisturizers. This may have been what I tasted every time I tried to sip my coffee.

My poop tube smelled bad, so they put fresh ground coffee under my bed to mask the odor. This may have triggered the scene where I purchase fresh ground coffee to be brewed for my consumption.

I was so restless I could hardly contain my flailing legs, so they had to restrain me. All these facts lay the foundation for this coma dream.

Coma Dream

The aroma of fresh ground coffee was wafting up from the coffee bins. Contemplating which bean would give the richest taste for a freshly brewed coffee, I finally settled on the dark bold French roast. Scooping out just enough beans from the bin, I proceeded to the checkout line and waited patiently for my selection to be ground and brewed.

The scent of freshly ground coffee was intense. It put me in a happy mood. My mom said she was going home now because I was doing much better. I was excited about leaving Mitchell and going home myself, back to Miami. It had been a long time since I had been home in my own bed.

The empty 1970s Greyhound bus looked out of place parked in front of the small-town grocery store in Mitchell. I was the first passenger to board, and I slowly made my way up the steps and down the aisle to the third row on the right. With a cup of coffee in one hand and an umbrella hooked over the arm carrying an overnight bag, I awkwardly slid into the firm cushioned seats. My anticipation of being able to finally relax and sip a great cup of coffee was greeted with disappointment.

The coffee did not taste like it should. It was terrible. What was this strange taste?

I looked down at my black umbrella—the big kind, not those cheap, convenient, portable types. Holding the wood handle, I began to spin the umbrella on its pointed metal tip, seeking an answer to my coffee mystery. Mesmerized by the twirling spoke tips, my mind went blank and my fingers grew tired of directing the handle round and round. The zipper on my overnight bag was half-opened, exposing sun lotion and water repellant for fabric and leather products.

"Is that what I'm tasting, one of those products?" Reaching into my bag, I pulled out the water repellant. I took off the lid and rolled it over my lips just to get a taste. Sweeping my dry tongue over my top lip, I paused a second to register the experience. *Wet, a bit gooey, a tad minty, and on the cool side,* I thought. It definitely had the same bizarre taste. I knew the water repellant was to waterproof my shoes and umbrella for the rainy season in Miami, but why would my coffee have the same flavor?

I accepted it because there was nothing I could do to make my beverage taste like coffee. Pressing my face against the cold glass bus window and focusing on my trip, I wondered how many passengers would be boarding the bus. Would I be all alone on this journey back to Miami? How many stops would we have on the way there? Did I have enough food packed in my overnight bag?

I waited for what seemed like hours for the driver to depart the IGA store station in Mitchell. Alone on this big empty bus, restlessness set in and claimed my legs. Twitching and jumping, my lower half seemed to take on a life of its own. The good news was I was going home. The bad news: I could not sit still.

The Worldly

It is tempting to conclude that somewhere in her psyche, Barbara was aware that she was coming out of her coma. Perhaps she knew that she was "going home." If that were the case, her apprehension is understandable. Loneliness and restlessness are the predominant feelings as she starts out on another journey into the unknown. How is she going to cope?

11

BAD PILOT

Barbara

Prelude to the Coma Dream

Somehow, in my coma, I had accurately remembered that my best friend was scheduled to fly in from Vancouver on December 9 for a week to visit me. However, in real time, it wasn't December 9; it was just before Thanksgiving, a detail that eluded my current reality. My son, looking forward to seeing her, had remembered this trip and had my sister call her and cancel.

I wonder if that's why I had remembered it: because I overheard Carl and Chris talk about it. This scenario became the theme for this coma dream.

Also, a male nurse who had an English accent removed the femoral catheter for dialysis from my groin. He asked my sister to hold pressure on the exit wound to stop the bleeding. The pain was excruciating and caused me to flail my legs, which also plays out in this dream.

Coma Dream

She lived in Vancouver and nobody knew her like me. She was my best friend since ninth grade. We had been staying in touch over the past three decades by email, phone, and the occasional visit. My anticipation for her December 9, 2009 visit was all I could think about. The years had been good to her; she was tall, blonde, and slender, boasting sultry eyes and a gorgeous smile. She knew all my secrets and life stories, as I knew hers.

Now a sociology professor, she always had something intelligent to say, especially when it came to our past male relationships. We could laugh and talk for hours and pick up right where we left off from conversations that happened years earlier.

It was December 9, and I had arranged to pick her up from the Miami Airport. It was a long flight from Vancouver, so any delay on my part was not an option.

However, on this particular day, something was wrong. Finding myself in a tiny remote airport somewhere, I realized I was not in Miami anymore. A young woman sitting at her desk was the only person in the small, dimly-lit interior room inside the hangar.

"Excuse me, ma'am," I interrupted. Her focus was fixed on the computer screen. She was slow to acknowledge my presence. Her head moved upward at a snail's pace. The glasses halfway down her nose and her straight black hair pulled tightly into a ponytail made her appear older than she was. She was in blue scrubs with a stethoscope draped around her neck, and she seemed annoyed by my presence.

Anxiety churned in my stomach as her lack of enthusiasm to respond was replaced by obvious apathy. However, it gave me enough time to consider a new plan: *If I charter a twin-engine turbo prop and pick her up myself, it would solve the problem*

"Miss Morello, what can we do for you?" she grumbled.

"I need to pick up my friend," I announced. "She needs to be informed immediately that I'll be picking her up in Vancouver instead of Miami. When is the next charter flight to Vancouver?"

She switched her attention from typing to placing medications into small paper cups. Then she looked straight at me and said, "Miss Morello, you won't be going anywhere tonight; you need to stay put."

"You don't understand," I said impatiently. "I need to pick her up in Vancouver. She'll be waiting for me." A desperate battle raged in my head. This woman seems to think she was in control. *What authority does she have over the situation, or me?*

"Miss Morello, it would be too risky to fly across the country at night in a twin prop," she said indignantly.

Every nerve humming with frustration told me to lash back at her unwillingness to cooperate. Her unfriendly gaze challenged my integrity.

I can deal with this, I assured myself while struggling to free my limbs

99

body from a sofa. Fumbling for words, I said, "I'm not waiting for the morning. Where is the pilot? I'll ask him myself."

A man with an English accent entered and said, "Miss Morello, the flying conditions are not favorable if we leave right now. As the pilot of this aircraft, I will not jeopardize our safety because of your impatience."

"Please," I pleaded. "I'm ready to go, and she'll be waiting for us."

He shook his head, cleared his throat, and said, "Miss Morello, I've had enough of your complaining."

My stubbornness must have enraged him. The night seemed to be closing in, stealing the last shade of gray offered through the window. The man clenched his fist. With the quickness of a striking snake, he punched me in the groin and knocked me back onto the sofa.

I screamed in disbelief, "What did you do that for?"

"That will teach you," he said. "Now stay put."

I felt as though a knife had been jammed and twisted into my flesh. It stunned me into submission, as every nerve burning and recoiling from the excruciating pain rendered me a prisoner. I was done. I felt like a pursued creature submitting to its predator after the crippling death bite.

The woman from behind the desk hovered over me and said, "Here, take this medication; it will help with the pain."

It wasn't the medication she had been dispensing earlier; it was some weird-tasting liquid. It was almost as if she knew I would be in this condition.

For a moment, no one spoke. A burst of adrenalin shot straight through my frail body, causing my legs to flail up and down. I wasn't sure if it was my body's way of dealing with the pain or my determination to get off the sofa and fly the plane myself.

"Now you for sure can't fly in this condition, because the altitude will cause you to bleed to death. Miss Morello, I suggest you stop squirming and lie still."

"What have you done?" I screamed.

"You need to hold her down," the pilot said as he released his grip on my leg.

"Now, Barb, hold still," bellowed the voice of my sister. *What is she doing here?* I wondered. *Is she in on this plot to take me down as well?* could feel her hands holding my right leg down. "Hold still, Barb," she commanded.

I was stunned when I heard, "Listen to your sister." That voice belonged to her boyfriend.

What's he doing here? Is he in on it too? When this is all over, I'm going to report this bad pilot to the FAA and have his license revoked. And I will never forgive my sister and her boyfriend for collaborating with this nasty man.

NOTE: It took me a couple of weeks to get over my anger for my sister from this scenario. I was actually convinced that she held my leg down after the supposed Bad Pilot punched me in the groin. I really believed she was in on a plan to hurt me and stop me from flying to pick up my best friend.

Howard

The Worldly

It is easy to speculate that as Barbara was coming out of her coma, she was restless and trying to get out of her bed, forcing the medical team to restrain her. Somehow, she remembered her friend's visit and was determined to take control.

Control. We all seek it and even need it. Feeling out of control is the toxic element of stress. It is so important to feel in control that we are much more comfortable creating false narratives than having no narrative at all. It is much more comfortable being wrong than lost. Control: that was what Barbara was reclaiming in her life after two weeks without the sense of being entitled to it.

12

WAKING UP

Barbara

The notes showed...well, never mind the notes. This was the day finally woke up! The male nurse with the English accent was on duty an my sister and Mike were there to watch me emerge.

REALITY

I took a deep breath of chilly air. I could feel the firm mattres supporting my body, but this time, it was different. I could reall move my limbs. My mind actually connected with my physical being *How liberating,* I thought. Though groggy, my curiosity was not inhibited

Where am I? What year is this? Actually, I don't even know who I an. Being unable to recollect what got me here in the first place was a littl unsettling. However, knowing the world of the living existed and I was i it created a sense of wellbeing. It must be how newborn babies fee entering into a cold, bright world, knowing they are missing the warmth c a dark, comfortable place, but experiencing the awareness of existenc There is no concept of time, place, or who and what you are—ju: existing.

The cool air caused me to snuggle under my sheets. My clumsy hands could barely communicate with unresponsive fingertips as I tried to adjust the sheets. Awkwardly forcing my hands upon my abdomen, I noticed something strange. What was this contraption? It felt like a belt had been fastened to my abdomen with clips and safety pins. *This must be how people come these days, with built-in belts,* I thought while trying to understand what this could possibly be used for.

The overhead fluorescent lights created a halo effect around the perimeter of the room. My eyes were squinting through what seemed like a haze. I could barely make out the figures dressed in blue that floated around effortlessly on the other side of the large doorway that spanned from wall to wall. Everything my eye focused on seemed fragmented, like looking through perforated metal.

Background noises like typing, ringing phones, talking people, and weird beeping noises conjured up images of being in a resort. The TV was on low. Listening intently, I wondered if there would be clues as to what day or time it was. The knocking sound of metal pipes contracting and expanding, like the sounds a house radiator makes as hot water cools, created the notion that I was in a cold climate at a ski resort.

I couldn't just lie there anymore. I needed to explore the room and look for clues. I fumbled as I tried to figure out a way of freeing myself from this bed.

Then, a man with a South African accent (which I thought was an English accent) said, "Miss Morello, you are not going anywhere. You need to stay put. You are really starting to get on my nerves. Now lay back down, or I'll have to tie your hands to the bed and keep you restrained."

He wore blue scrubs and hovered over me. I could see only one eye and some black hair. That was when I realized my vision was impaired. He appeared to be tall, but he was missing parts of his body. He seemed to float around without legs. But I remembered that accent. He was the "Bad Pilot."

I felt like a prisoner on death row sitting blindfolded in the electric chair. There was no escape from this evil man. My memory flashed back to the excruciating pain he'd inflicted on my groin with the help of my sister. Then I wondered what happened to my girlfriend. Who picked her up?

A commercial for Atlantis was on TV. The sugary sands, warm breezy air, breathtaking sunset, and crystal clear turquoise water showcased a paradise for anyone desiring a perfect getaway destination. The image of a pineapple and tropical resort registered a positive response with my tired mind. *That's it. I'm in the Bahamas at a resort waiting for my friend to join me.* With that realization, I began to become sleepy, drifting in and out of consciousness.

The next thing I realized, somebody was asking me to open my eyes.

"She's smiling," came the very excited voice of my sister. "Look Mike, she's smiling."

What's wrong with these people? I thought. *You want to see a smile, watch this.* With every ounce of strength I had, I cracked a smile that stretched across my face. It seemed to amuse everyone in the room. *Is the*

105

all it takes to get people's attention? I wondered.

Finally finding myself back in the land of the living, I reconnected with my family. I was so happy to be alive, but I realized that I was somehow different. For starters, my voice was gone and communication was limited to a whisper. I was told the tubes in my throat from the life support machine caused this, but not to worry, as my voice would soon return. My limbs and hands moved so awkwardly, and I was unable to remember anything. Carla handed me my cell phone, and I couldn't figure out why it was so heavy. It felt like it weighed at least twenty pounds. *Strange,* I thought. *Have I become that weak, or do phones weigh more now?*

Soon after I came out of the coma, my cardiologists entered the room. "Good morning, Barbara," came a somber voice. "How are you doing this morning?"

Hardly able to contain my excitement, I muttered, "You wouldn't believe it. I met an angel who took me to an amazing place. He healed my heart."

His look was one of concern. "Barbara, that's a nice story, but there has been talk about putting you on a heart transplant list or getting you a mechanical heart. You have gone through a lot. But just to entertain your story, let's have an ultrasound done and see if your angel story is right."

After the ultrasound was done, he waltzed into my room.

He looked at me intently, and after a long pause, made his announcement.

"This is truly a miracle. Your heart is just fine. In fact, your heart could be used for someone else requiring a heart transplant."

The doctor had just given me some great news. He had literally confirmed my new lease on life.

At that moment, sensations of hope and encouragement surged through my body. I felt that my death sentence had been averted and I was given a second chance.

In that instant, everything changed.

I reached instinctively for my panic button to summon a nurse. One quickly arrived.

"Please," I asked with urgency, "Is there a chaplain or priest in the hospital that can visit with me?"

The nurse said she would find someone. I was like a kid in a candy store, as I wanted to talk about God and my experience with someone in a spiritual profession.

I asked for anyone available that day so I could share my story and get his feedback because I felt like I had been in the presence of God. Every day, I begged the nurses to send me a chaplain, pastor, minister, reverend, deacon—anyone that would help me find out more about my experience.

For the first week, they did indeed send religious people to talk to me daily. We discussed my experience and prayed, but underneath it all, I was also still scared that I was going to die. I wanted reassurance that in the event of death, I was going to go to the right place. Perhaps the memory of Satan loomed too large. I had only lost two weeks of my life, but losing two weeks of conscious time made me think. The year was 2009, and mankind had been around for thousands of years. So why were we only in 2009 and not 15009 or 20009? Then it hit me: the birth of Jesus was so significant that it denoted the date system. A.D. stands for "anno domini," Latin for "in the year of the lord," and refers specifically to the birth of Jesus Christ. "B.C." stands for "before Christ."

If the birth of Jesus was so significant as to establish the date standard for the entire world, how is it the world does not recognize Him? I felt like I had just spent a day with Him in God's waiting room and He was very real, as was my miraculous healing. I wanted to shout this from the rooftops or to anyone who cared to listen.

While I was awakening spiritually, I still had physical concerns. After coming so close to death, fear remained. After all, I still was not in the clear from the numerous complications. All the weight gained from the liquids pumped into my body while on life support was slowly draining off. Every other day, I endured the tedious five-hour process of sitting in an uncomfortable wheelchair while having dialysis. Feeling nauseated was a side effect from the process. Clutching my barf bag, I wondered how much longer I would have to endure this.

My nephrologist was a sweet and gentle man. Looking at me through his kind eyes, he delivered the bad news. "Barbara, I hate to tell you, but you'll have a more permanent dialysis port installed. Your kidneys will never be able to function on their own. We may consider a kidney transplant down the road if they get worse."

"What?" I cried out in my whispery voice. *No way; this is not going to happen to me. There is no way I'm living life this way. There will be* *another miracle and my kidneys will return to normal.* "Please," I begged "do not install that port."

The next thing I knew, I was laying on a cold steel table staring up at a bright light and a pair of eyes. The knife poised just above my right breast close to the shoulder slowly pushed into my skin, as the doctor was installing the dialysis port. *I thought they said I would be out for this procedure, so why am I still awake?* I thought. Flashbacks of the coma suddenly shook me into fear. *Maybe I'm trapped in my body again.* Panic swept over me as I felt very cold and exposed. *Will this ordeal ever end?* I wondered.

Finding myself back in the confines of my hospital room, I noticed blood seeping through my hospital gown where the port had been installed. Hours later, it looked like I had been knifed. Blood was everywhere. Just then, in walked a reiner friend of mine who happened to work at the hospital. She seemed to magically appear every time I was in distress, and this was one of those occasions. The doctor was called in to stop the bleeding. My blood was not coagulating. There was concern as the doctor worked hard on packing the wound with white blood cell platelets. The packing process was very painful. My dear friend was such a comfort as she held my hand.

As I was still very helpless and frail, a physical therapist was brought in daily to help me use my hands and learn to walk and breathe. Atrophy had impaired my muscles and breathing was difficult. Twice daily, I was given the CPAP and breathing exercises. I wondered if I would ever be

109

able to breathe effectively on my own again. Taking my first few steps seemed difficult. Mike was cheering me on. "Come on, baby, you can do it." As I put one foot in front of the other while pushing a walker, I thought, *Is this what it feels like to be a ninety-year-old?* It was as if I had never walked before. Slowly, over the next three weeks, I made progress.

It was just before Christmas, and the hospital was decorated in full splendor. Mike's niece, Kaleigh, brought me an adorable, small, decorated Christmas tree for my room. The thoughtful gift brightened my remaining days at the hospital and created a beautiful bonding moment.

It had been five long weeks since being admitted on November 14th. The hospital released me December 18th, and I will never forget leaving the hospital. I was excited to go home, yet terrified that my condition could get worse. I was told I would be in recovery for the next two years from the trauma that my organs had sustained. I still felt very sick.

13

RECOVERY

Barbara

Leaving the hospital, I was in a fog. Mike was finally bringing m⌐ home. I was disoriented, and my reality rested somewhere betwee⌐ the Coma Dreams and the present. Would I ever be free from th⌐ post-traumatic stress? As queasiness evolved into full-blown nausea, realized my vision was adjusting to the outside world while in motior⌐ Bits and pieces of cars, trees, the street, and homes flickered in and ou⌐ through a haze. *Am I still stuck in a bad dream or is this for real?* As looked at Mike while he drove, I realized he too appeared to be in bits an⌐ pieces. How would I recognize him in a crowd? Questions were filling m⌐ head, and I had no answers. Not knowing the full extent of the brai⌐ damage from my stroke left me questioning my future.

Amidst all the confusion, I knew Mike loved me. Without his love an⌐ support as my advocate and prayer warrior, I don't know if I would hav⌐ pulled through. As we rolled into the driveway, he reminded me that ou⌐ pet pups, Bosco and Tyra, really missed me.

"Who?" I said, mystified. *That's funny,* I thought. I could n⌐

remember who or what they were. Actually, I had no memory of them at all. I stepped down from the truck and Mike helped me walk into our home. Forcing myself to breathe left me out of air with every step in my frail and weakened state from muscle atrophy. Eight paws and two tails pattered around me as I stepped through the door. Yes, it was slowly coming back to me. It was all I could do to trudge over to the sofa at snail's pace while dancing, excited dogs were happy to see me.

While I was thrilled to be home with family and pets, it was just too much activity in one day. I was dizzy, weak, and nauseated. I lay my head down and curled up in a ball, getting the sense this was not going to be an easy recovery. With only seven days left before Christmas, I wondered how I would get my shopping done.

During these weeks, as I emerged from my coma, I knew that my life had changed dramatically and that a continued spiritual transformation lay ahead of me. However, I also knew that my first goal was survival and regaining some of my physical capabilities. I was visually impaired, could barely walk, and had difficulty speaking and even hearing, and every cell in my body needed time to heal.

I needed to put in a lot of work to turn my miracle into my mission. I knew at the level of my soul that I was on the verge of something meaningful, and I couldn't wait to start to explore and manifest it. But first, I had to recover enough of my physical strength and faculties to function.

In my sick and weak state, the sofa became my new home, with me only moving from it to use the bathroom. For the first week, it took every ounce of breath and energy just to get to the bathroom and back. While in the bathroom, I peered into my makeup mirror. I was unable to see both eyes at the same time, and the eye that could be seen was also broken down into fragments. *Freaky,* I thought while studying my new image in the mirror. I could not even recognize myself. I felt as broken as my fragmented vision.

Feeling restless and unsettled, I had a flashback to the hospital. The last five weeks had been no picnic. Lying in a bed with painful bedsores, bored out of my mind, reminded me that being home was luxury. There was no one prodding me with needles and taking my temperature every hour. Indeed, I could finally get some rest. By now, everyone had grown weary of catering to my needs. It forced me to exert myself more than had been. I was thin and frail, and my clothes didn't fit me anymore. With a gaunt face and sagging muscles, I forced myself to fight the fight and get my old self back. I had once been the poster child for fitness, health, and positive attitude.

As I struggled to get through the Christmas holidays, there were some improvements in my strength. I could actually hold my phone and squeeze a soft foam ball. I was still unable to reach the goal required for breathing exercises, but determination powered my will. We take the act of breathing for granted, and I never imagined it could be this difficult. The real test was going to be my computers. I completely forgot how to use both my Mac and PC. Starting back at square one, I had no clue. How could this be? I had used my computers for over twenty years. But wasn't just that; I could not remember how to do anything I had done before. Even a simple task like writing a check did not compute. I knew in my head what I wanted to write, but it did not translate to paper. Did I have Alzheimer's? What was going on? Did the stroke cause that much damage?

The realization of my losses overwhelmed me. Mentally, I was damaged, physically, I was equivalent to an eighty-year-old, and visually, I was struggling with the challenges of sight. I could not return to my profession. Defined by being an architectural rendering artist, I was lost. Who was I? My rock star status had come to a screeching halt. At that moment, the reality of what I had become hit me.

The first week in January, my mom agreed to fly down from Canada to help me adjust to my new life. I asked for her help with small tasks like writing checks. Little did we know at the time, but vascular dementia was already ailing my mom. She, too, was unable to write out a simple check. It was like the blind leading the blind. Alarmed by her deterioration, I wondered if I was going to be like her. Would I get better or worse?

My mom, who was proficient at walking, suggested we set a new goal in distance every day. The first day, I could barely walk 200 yards due to breathing difficulties and atrophy, but by the end of the week, I managed our neighborhood block. Though still very slow, my muscles were gradually strengthening, and by the third week, I was victorious in walking half a mile. Taking several breaks along the way allowed me to handle such an undertaking.

Relearning my computer skills was a daunting task, but slowly, one day at a time, I was able to recall what had been lost. Unfortunately, this

114

process took a couple of years. To this day, I'm extremely slow when using the programs, making many mistakes. With technology came helpful tools like speech-to-text and text-to-speech software, which facilitated reading emails and documents.

In February, seven weeks into my recovery, the challenges of daily life were setting in. Tripping over dogs, curbs, speed bumps, small children, or just about anything from the waist down left me with constant bruises. Difficulties with speech, memory loss, facial recognition, and flashback of my coma were discouraging. I was still feeling the effects of the H1N flu, and the high blood pressure and damage sustained by the stage-three kidney disease produced very itchy skin and exhaustion, which wasn't fun. Feeling nauseated most days, I continued to lose weight. And that's not the only thing I lost. By the end of March, I had lost most of my thick beautiful hair, leaving me devastated. My sister Carla had recently visited me in the beginning of March, witnessing my losses, but her presence was comforting. The good news was the dialysis port was removed in January, as my kidneys somehow improved enough that I no longer needed to be on dialysis.

Finally, at the end of March, I started back at the gym. Walking slowly on the treadmill for ten minutes became my starting point. Being barely able to complete that task reminded me of how far I had already come. Though I was out of breath, I knew it could only get better. I was using the lightest weights and slowly doing exercises to stimulate muscle growth and my improvements were encouraging me. I wasn't able to engage the muscle in my left arm, atrophied by the stroke, meaning I needed some

115

physical therapy. The arm was painful and awkward to maneuver, and to this day I do not have full use of it.

By June, with very little hair, I hit my goal of walking thirty minutes on the treadmill. And slowly, over time, I regained my lung capacity and full head of hair, as well as the ability to do physical exercises that I previously took for granted. My life was slowly getting back on track, but it was obvious that I would never be the same person I was before the stroke. I had to figure out how to reinvent myself. But before I could do that, time was needed to both physically and mentally heal.

The following year, with my newfound desire to grow in faith and embrace the grace that was extended to me on my deathbed, I began bible study classes. My friend Tessie, who runs a gym in Miami, held these classes once a week over the summer. It was like being parched in the hot sun and diving into a juicy piece of watermelon and having my thirst quenched. It made me want more.

Then, my other friend, Beth, urged me to try Bible Study Fellowship (BSF) for a year. It has literally transformed my life. Over the past seven years of doing both studies, as well as participating in small groups through our church, I have been given an understanding of scripture that I had never known before. I had no idea the Bible was so rich and steeped in history, and so relevant to today's cultural challenges. My first volunteer work was taking flowers with a friend of mine from BSF to a nearby hospital. After giving the floral arrangements to the patients, we would offer prayer to comfort them if they wanted it.

Knowing the incredible healing power of horses, I slowly got back in the saddle. At first, balance presented a challenge, but the more I rode, the better my comfort level and balance got. These majestic creatures were responsible for much of my recovery—mentally, physically, and emotionally. I spent the next years honing my horsemanship skills as well as volunteering at a residential treatment facility in Miami. Using faith based principles, we would do fun and spontaneous creative art. It was a wonderful way of healing, finding purpose, and learning about having a relationship with God.

6 YEARS LATER

As I was looking for a ghostwriter to help write my story, I realized Howard Rankin was the perfect fit when he shared his behavioral science background and his faith testimonial. He understood that I was still suffering from posttraumatic stress. Howard is a good listener and was able to shed deep insight, helping me process the coma experiences. He is not only a writer, but a man who understands the inner workings of the brain. It was clearly a match made in Heaven. Together, we embarked on an incredible journey of discovery and healing.

I had no idea how much my past was connected with my Coma Dreams, and this was the way my brain processed unresolved issues. The next year was spent writing this book with a new understanding of how the brain works. With every chapter, Howard had the ability and perception to help me understand how it related to unresolved issues from my past. With this, we could talk in depth about the events in my coma and how they were manifested from real life events that took place in my past. The coma and meeting Howard had proven to be a tremendous blessing in my life. Healing issues is the key to being able to move forward.

7 YEARS LATER

Given my lifelong connection and experience riding horses, I found he unconditional love of these animals to be healing, both physically and emotionally. I felt privileged to have had horses during my childhood and or the past eighteen years. With my second chance at life, See Horse was founded as a faith-based non-profit organization. See Horse provides women and youth with equine-assisted learning and recreation, so they too can find healing, hope, and purpose in their lives. My need of purpose, ove of horses, and a desire to serve has made See Horse the perfect fit for me.

Over the past few years, I have not only enjoyed giving back to ociety, but have learned how to work with horses in a way that is very different from when I was competing. When in competition, a trainer was ired to maintain and prepare my horse for the reining events. Because of my demanding work schedule, I only had time to practice once or twice er week. I have always bonded with my horses, but this time around, it was different. With more time available, I trained my own horses with methods learned from renowned horse whisperers using natural orsemanship techniques and experience accumulated from my past horse ainers.

Focusing on the importance of building and strengthening relationships with horses has taught me how to communicate and witness incredible results with their willingness to interact and perform. It is this communication that enables me to understand what they are thinking and feeling. Being so in tune with my horses has allowed me to realize they have the same emotional traits as humans. In fact, they have seventeen different facial gestures that depict their emotions, while humans have twenty-seven. Their body language also reflects their intentions, thoughts and reactions to humans, other horses, and environmental elements.

Using horses for animal-assisted learning is a great tool for uncovering and breaking down the layers of walls that people surround themselves with. Horses mirror our distrust, feelings of insecurities, impatience, impulsiveness, aggressiveness, disconnection with others, sadness, and abandonment issues. Horses don't lie and react honestly according to what they are sensing with the individual. We can safely explore a person's past while they are interacting with the horse. The individual is asked to perform certain tasks with the horse. By paying attention to the horse's reactions, questions and comments are presented to the individual. This leads to self-discovery and reflection intended to help reveal hidden issues or abilities in a relaxed and fun environment.

As the individual's issue is being revealed, faith-based principles are discussed to help them understand how God can work in their lives if they let Him. We close out in prayer, asking God to replace their exposed issues with healing, and for Him to help them rewrite their narratives with something constructive. Reinforcing the power of prayer and having relationship with Jesus as a way to make transformation possible is an essential part of this session. Every time we do equine-assisted learning, my volunteer partners, Joel Ann Shiffer, Tina Smith, Chaplain Laura, and Hayse Chamoun, and I feel somehow touched, and we are able to apply the lesson to our own lives. This form of learning has been a powerful tool for transformation.

One of the key points we impress on the individuals is, "we become the company we keep." The survival of horses that live in the wild depends upon the cooperation of the herd. One bad horse will jeopardize the wellbeing of the entire herd. Because they are prey animals, they are subject to predators like bobcats and mountain lions. The leading horse will oust the uncooperative horse just to keep the herd safe. Therefore, we strongly urge the women and youth to pick their friends with discernment, or trouble will surely follow. This applies in particular to individuals suffering from substance abuse.

The most profound thing that I have learned through my coma experience and doing equine-assisted learning is that our souls need a power source to successfully thrive. We need to plug in every morning as we plug in our cell phones to recharge the batteries. Without recharging the batteries, our cell phones are of little use to us. The same is true if we do not recharge the batteries of our soul; we will have trouble operating in life.

I have now found a new way of living through plugging in: being in a relationship with Jesus that brings about the peace, joy, love, and wisdom that transcends all worldly understanding. "Plugging in" simply means

120

praying. There is such a desperate need for people of prayer in this world of atheism and anti-Christian practices. I believe God is calling His people to prayer more intensively than ever before. If we could only comprehend the immensity of God's plan for our lives, and the importance of our prayers, we would stop in our tracks and reevaluate our priorities immediately. Life is just too short and too precious to waste on empty things. As I write this, I can't help but think of the tremendous prayers that were poured out for me while being in the coma. Was it because of the intercession on my behalf for a miraculous healing that God gave me a second chance?

None of us know how many days, weeks, or months we have left in this precious life. For example, I was diagnosed with breast cancer this year, but from all that I have learned through my coma experiences, I was able to deal with it surprisingly well.

14

COMA AND CONSCIOUSNESS

Howard

Barbara's experience tells us a lot, not just about being in a coma or about faith, but the very way our minds work. When her coma took away her consciousness and the higher workings of the mind, she was left with a brain that could process sensory information but not analyze it logically. Her experience shines a bright light on what consciousness is and how it works.

Although Barbara could "only" experience sensory input, what is remarkable is that the sensory input was still interpreted and associated with past experiences and elicited an emotional response. Her brain didn't just register the sensations, it made a story out of them—a story that was consistent and resonated with her past experiences. With the higher functions of her brain taken offline, she temporarily traveled back down the evolutionary trail.

Research in cognitive science over the past few decades has revealed much about the way the human mind works. In his excellent book *Thinking, Fast and Slow,* psychologist Daniel Kahneman, who won the Nobel Prize for Economics for his contribution to Behavioral Economics, describes two types of thinking. System 1 thinking is what we think of as intuition and "gut feel." It is based on past experiences, memories, our narratives, and the lens through which we characteristically see the world. System 2 thinking is much more demanding and involves rational, logical analysis. Most people depend on System 1 thinking with a cursory nod in the direction of rational analysis. Of course, we think we're being logical and we can always create a story that justifies our stories. But a lot of the time, the basis for our thoughts and decisions lies with this gut feel approach.

Barbara's coma experiences show how easily our brains can create a powerful story that seems completely real to us at the time. These subconscious processes are in play whether we are in or out of a coma. Our brains react to events by unconsciously creating powerful stories that shape our experience and influence us significantly. Barbara's story is testimony to the fact that perhaps one of the most important things we need to learn is that the brain will generate stories in an instant. It is therefore critical for us to use higher mental processes to evaluate those stories and match them against reality. These stories genuinely have the power to become our reality, and so it is important that we make the attempt to rationally evaluate them. And the fact is that it is easier to accept them than to analyze them critically.

Barbara's story, therefore, isn't just about a coma; it is about the challenge we all face in needing to be aware of the narratives our brains produce and the need to critically analyze them. Otherwise, while you may be responsive, you might effectively be in a coma. Think of the power of the emotion that had Barbara convinced she was going to get a bill from Caribou Electric Company long after she had regained consciousness and could even acknowledge the notion was absurd. If the emotion and the narrative are strong enough, logic doesn't have much of a chance.

However, all of that notwithstanding, a balance between System 1 intuition and System 2 rationality is the ideal. Despite the fact that we can be rational, the fact is that the human brain is limited. It filters and processes senses through the lens of its own restricted capabilities. As human beings, we can only "know" so much. The rest depends on perspective and faith.

So, was Barbara's encounter with an angel simply a metaphor? It certainly has metaphorical significance, but it wasn't "just a metaphor." In fact, in this case, she was able to validate what the angel told her. She did indeed see through different eyes when she emerged from the coma. And an independent cardiologist confirmed through scientific measurement that her heart had recovered its function and was now in excellent shape.

Think about Barbara's story. She escaped the boundaries of her own ego by resolving many of her life issues. When we are not driven by our egos, we are then open to developing a spiritual connection. It's hard to escape the clutches of our egos; we want too much. We want love, money, success, and appreciation, and when we want, the ego dictates. Giving up the ego is not easy, especially in an ego-driven society that is based on creating and fulfilling wants. Escaping the ego is scary, but the rewards are amazing. What happens when you escape your ego and stop wanting, and start appreciating and loving? Barbara was able to do this, and when she did, amazing things happened. She was told she would have meaning as well as get a healed heart and a new perspective on life. She has found that meaning and purpose through helping others who are, in a way trapped in their own form of coma. Now she is performing the role of the pediatric angel, giving hope, guidance, and inspiration to help other resolve their issues, find connection, and literally have "a change of heart" about the direction of their lives. The ego-driven search is over; now she can be filled with gratitude, love, and peace.

In some ways, it doesn't surprise me that Barb's transformation happened in a coma. Perhaps that was the only place it could happen. If she were conscious, she would have been distracted by a million things that probably would have prevented her from fully focusing on the rewrite of her script. More importantly, she would have been locked into habitual thoughts and doubts—a prisoner to her life's narrative. The essence of wisdom and enlightenment is to be able to shake off the shackles of our narratives and thinking habits and see ourselves in a new light. This is a very difficult task when those very stories are the lenses through which you are looking at yourself and the world.

15

TRANSFORMATION

Howard

C hange is an inevitable part of life. In fact, life is change. Every encounter with destiny challenges us to reshape our lives and legacies. Every encounter forces us down new paths that lead to more uncertainty. The neuroscience research clearly shows that the brain changes in structure whenever we adapt and learn, especially when we deal with challenges. Moreover, each step of the way is an opportunity for more growth and spiritual development.

In his book *Rediscover Jesus,* the brilliant Matthew Kelly writes about how most of us want tweaks to our lives—an improvement here, more money there, a better house, a newer car—but most of us don't want what we really need: a major transformation. As a result, we can feel disappointed and unfulfilled. As Kelly writes on page 85:

"We pray for tweaking, then wonder why God doesn't answer our prayers. The reason is simple: God is not in the business of tweaking. He is in the business of transformation."

When transformations do occur, they often happen because of our own failings—or events that we would consider "negative," but are actually liberating. "Sometimes God lets you hit rock bottom so that you will discover that He is the rock at the bottom," writes Dr. Tony Evans

People see their challenges and "rock bottom" as negative events. I don't. I see rock bottom as the place where you finally face the fact that "being in control" is an illusion. It's scary, but also liberating.

In the health sciences, there are many examples of individuals who have overcome unlikely odds to defy ghastly medical prognoses. My book *Inspired to Lose,* which chronicled the stories of thirty-five people trying to lose significant amounts of weight, includes the story of Fran Drozdz. Fran turned to her faith and not only survived but has run marathons in every state and Washington D.C. in the thirty-five years since her "remission."

There are some compelling individual case studies about the relationship between faith, love, and recovery. Stanford's David Speigel initially set out to show that support groups really add nothing to the chances of recovery for women with cancer, but his data showed the enormous value of support, both in terms of length and quality of life, and focused researchers' attention on psychological and spiritual aspects of health. Dean Ornish, a famous cardiologist and lifestyle expert, says in his book *Love and Survival* that love, in its broadest terms, is the key factor in recovery from heart disease. Even as far back as the 19th century, a famous British Doctor, William Osler, suggested that the treatment of tuberculosis had more to do "with what the patient had on his mind, rather than on what he had on his chest."

More than a hundred years after Osler, distinguished scientist and practitioner Candace Pert showed that emotions could be, and were, transmitted to every cell in the body, evaporating the artificial distinction between mind and body. As she says in her incredible book *Molecules of Emotion*, "Your body is your subconscious."

Barb's story is essentially one of spiritual transformation. Facing the ultimate challenge, she resolved her spiritual crises, and this enabled her to heal physically and emotionally. Her experience changed her life. It led her to become a teacher in a different sort of classroom—one where experience teaches the ultimate lessons of love, hope, and faith. She teaches not with the use of markers, boards, and flash cards, but from her heart and her experiences, and through the medium of magnificent animals—horses. Her lessons aren't about facts, but about the fundamentals of a spiritual life, and they are lessons we could all learn and should never tire of revisiting. They are the lessons of transformation.

Being a good Christian isn't easy. Sure, we can go to church, say our prayers, and try to avoid sinning, but there's something more. At a time when there are so many doubters and people leaving the church, it becomes even more imperative to live our lives exhibiting the joy of Christ's message. In his book *The Holy Longing: The Search for a Christian Spirituality,* Ronald Rolheiser writes:

"The last thing that Jesus asked of us before he ascended, was that we go to all people and nations and preach his presence. However, that must be understood precisely in an incarnational, not theistic, way. The challenge is not to pass out religious tracts, establish religious television networks to make Jesus known, or even try to baptize everyone into Christianity. The task is to radiate the compassion and love of God, as manifest Jesus, in our faces and our actions." (p.102)

Barbara now radiates that compassion.

16

THE BEAUTY OBSESSION

Howard

O ne of the key themes in this story is the role of self-perception of women in today's western and first world societies. As a modern woman, Barbara was raised in a culture of sexuality where looks were all-important and presented as the most critical characteristic for a girl to develop. These messages are covert and overt in our society, exacerbated and exaggerated by the media, and prevalent everywhere. The vast majority of girls today and in Barbara's era are told in one way or another that sexuality and attractiveness are the most important aspect of their identities. Cosmetics, clothes, and arguably almost everything else are designed or promoted with the sexual message in mind.

The extent of this influence was brought home to me recently while working on a book with a New Zealand academic who had spent about a year in Saudi Arabia. Expecting to find oppressed women forced to wear the traditional dark, concealing Muslim clothing, this academic found the opposite: liberated women who were freed from the cultural demand to flaunt their bodies and the imperative of making themselves as physically desirable as possible. The traditional clothing for these Muslim women wasn't a sign of male oppression—far from it. It was, for many, the opportunity to escape the rampant sexual demands implicit in western and many other cultures.

It is noteworthy that Barb's name is associated with the symbol of female beauty: the Barbie doll. Barbie's dimensions have been a hallmark of beauty since her introduction in the 1960s. However, like those of a photo-shopped anorexic model, those dimensions are not only unrealistic they are potentially deadly. A Yale study found that a typical woman would need to gain twenty-four inches in height, add five inches to her chest, and lose six inches around her waist to emulate the Barbie Doll's dimensions. Only one in 100,000 women would have these dimensions.

The power of the beauty/sex imperative runs throughout Barbara's narrative, but is best illustrated in her Record Ring Death sequence. Even though she knows the consequences are fatal, Barb still can't resist the idea of being irresistible. She has to be sexy or bust; or in this case, die. And, of course, in the next coma sequence, Satan's direct pitch was couched in terms of Barbara's loss of sexual appeal. "If you have no sex appeal, you have nothing," claims Satan.

Today, women in the western world at least have opportunities to manifest their skills and talents in many different ways. Sure, it's nice to be attractive, and there is a premium on beauty—for example, attractive men and women make more money than their less attractive counterparts—but too many women are defined, and define themselves primarily by their physical appearance. There's nothing wrong with being attractive but it's not the most important aspect of a woman's—or a man's—identity.

Women have fought long and hard to change the perception of their abilities and identities to something more than just a pretty face or sexy body. I am very happy to have helped chronicle the history of the All American Red Heads, an all-female basketball team that barnstormed North America and beyond from 1936-1986 playing and (more often than not) beating men's teams. *Breaking the Press; The Incredible Story of the All American Red Heads*[1] is the story of how these young women completely changed the perception of female physical fitness, competitiveness, sporting talent, and overall ability. They showed that women could compete with men without losing their femininity; they helped redefine feminine possibilities.

There is nothing inherently wrong in aspiring to be beautiful or feeling attractive, but there is something inherently wrong in thinking that physical appearance should define you. Unfortunately, Barb was trapped in that falsehood, and it almost cost her life itself. Fortunately for her, though, when confronted with that demonic idea, she was able to reject it and find a different sort of beauty. Beauty and attractiveness depend on vision, and it is interesting that Barb suffered a loss of vision as well as a sealed heart. I also know this: Barbara now cares less about how she looks and more about who she is.

Perhaps we all need to focus more on our hearts rather than our eyes.

THE END

Epilogue

"Barbara's story was to be one of miraculous recovery. Hers was the third case of influenza-induced cardiomyopathy we had seen that month. Of the other two, one had died and the other had been transferred to the University Hospital for cardiac transplant. There was no reason to believe that her case would fare any differently. She was in a coma, on a breathing machine, and on dialysis treatments since her kidneys had shut down. After ten days of being at death's door, she began to recover remarkably fast; by the end of two weeks, she was talking and off the breathing and dialysis machines. It was truly a miracle." —Dr. Jorge Busse, attending physician

References

Daniel Kahneman (2011). *Thinking, Fast and Slow.* Farrar- Strauss

Matthew Kelly (2015) *Rediscover Jesus.* Beacon Publishing.

Howard Rankin (2001). *Inspired to Lose.* Stepwise Press

Dean Ornish (1999). *Love and Survival: The Scientific Basis of the Healing Power of Intimacy.* Harper Collins

Candace Pert (2010). *Molecules of Emotion: The Science Behind Mind-Body Medicine.* Simon & Schuster

Ronald Rolheiser (2009) *The Holy Longing: The Search for a Christian Spirituality.* Doubleday

About Barbara Morello O'Donnell

As you have read, Barbara and Mike are now married and live in Miami, where Barbara continues to volunteer at a residential substance abuse treatment facility for women, utilizing See Horse Miami's equine-assisted learning program. For more about Barbara and her story, please visit www.InGodsWaitingRoom.net

About Howard Rankin

Howard Rankin is a full-time writer and coach. He has written eleven books in his own name, seven as a co-writer, and more than twenty-five others as a ghostwriter. His book *I Think Therefore I Am Wrong: Thoughts on Wisdom* is due out in 2018. You can find out more at www.psychologywriter.com.

SEE HORSE MIAMI

Since starting the faith-based See Horse Miami program, we've helped many women and youth not only find hope, healing, and purpose, but also self-awareness through the mirroring ability of horses. We talk about their discoveries and encourage them to rewrite their narratives, so they don't feel stuck in a place that keeps them using mind-numbing drugs and alcohol. We've seen how impactful equine-assisted therapy has been, so now we're on a quest to expand the program, reaching women of human trafficking abuse.

You can help us by donating to our non-profit, run exclusively by volunteers. Your donation will directly expand our capacity to serve and help us sustain our program operations. Healing is a community process; therefore, we have designed our campaign to include the names of all our donors in the See Horse sanctuary. Additionally, we provide the opportunity for you or a loved one to experience the magic of E.A.L. (equine-assisted learning) for yourself. Even if you don't plan to come to Miami to participate in the equine-assisted learning program, you can donate your session to one of our community partners. For more information on helping See Horse Miami, please visit our website.

Donations can be made online at www.seehorsemiami.org

Photos on the following pages are of some of the women and youth who participated in equine-assisted learning and recreation over the past five years.

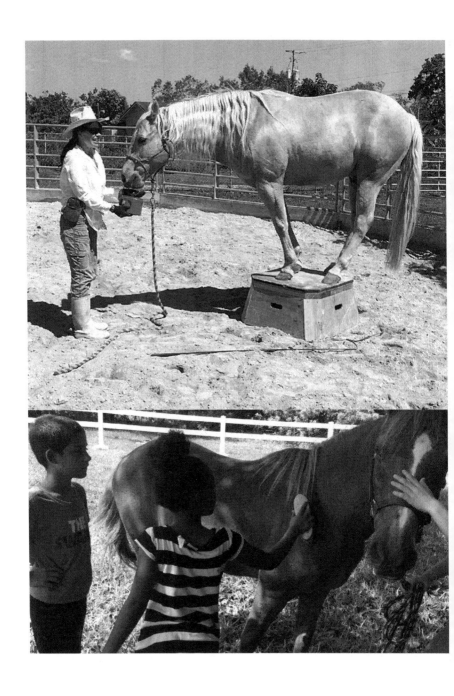

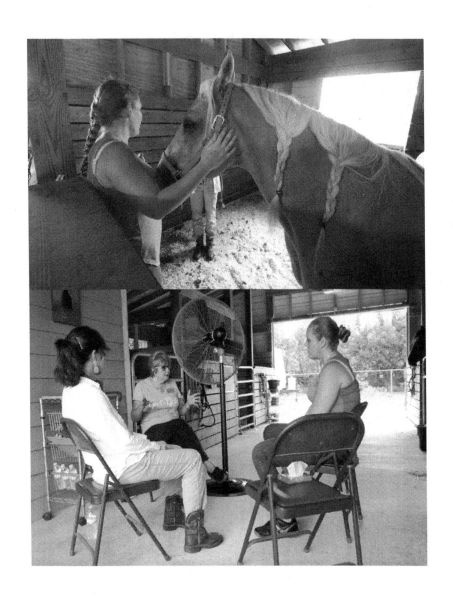

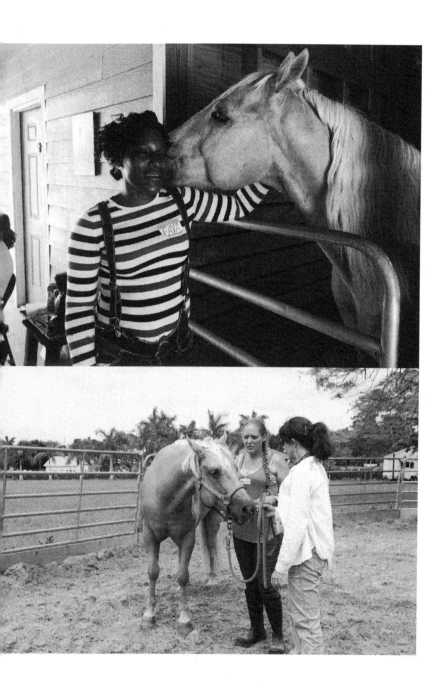

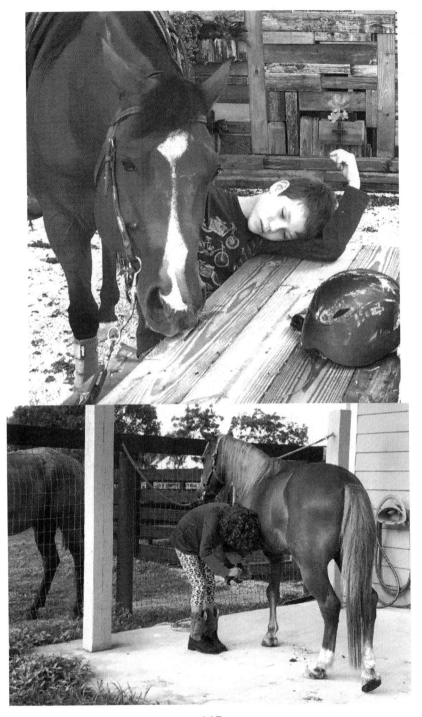

Made in the USA
Columbia, SC
18 May 2018